On Sacrifice

cs

On Sacrifice

જી

Moshe Halbertal

Princeton University Press
Princeton and Oxford

Copyright © 2012 by Princeton University Press
Published by Princeton University Press, 41 William Street,
Princeton, New Jersey 08540
In the United Kingdom: Princeton University Press, 6 Oxford Street,
Woodstock, Oxfordshire OX20 1TW

press.princeton.edu

Library of Congress Cataloging-in-Publication

Halbertal, Moshe.
On sacrifice / Moshe Halbertazl.
p. cm.
Includes biographical references (p.) and index.
ISBN 978-0-691-15285-1 (hardcover)
1. Sacrifice. 2. Self-sacrifice. I. Title.
BL570.H35 2012
203"4—dc23
2011037112

British Library Cataloging-in-Publication Data is available

This book has been composed in Sabon

Printed on acid-free paper. ∞

Printed in the United States of America

1   3   5   7   9   10   8   6   4   2

To the memory of my father,
Meir Halbertal

☙

Contents
ↃↃ

Acknowledgments
ↀ

I am deeply grateful to colleagues and friends who offered me their wisdom and support. The comments and insights of Gary Anderson, Hillel Ben-Sasson, Menachem Fisch, Toby Freilich, Stephen Holmes, Natalie Lithwick, Avishai Margalit, Richard Moran, Kimberley Patton, Amelie Rorty, Yishai Rozen-Zvi, Irit Samet, Michael Sandel, Seana Shiffrin, Dror Yinon, and the anonymous readers for Princeton University Press were most helpful.

Sections of the book were presented at the New York University Law School colloquium for legal, political, and social philosophy led by Ronald Dworkin and Thomas Nagel. I benefited a great deal from Dworkin's and Nagel's probing remarks as well as the engaging discussion with colloquium participants.

I wish to thank Fred Appel, my editor at Princeton University Press, for his encouraging support and advice, and the copy editor, Cindy Milstein, for her patient reading and valuable comments.

I am grateful to the New York University Filomen D'Agostino Foundation for the grants which supported the writing of the book.

On Sacrifice

ↄ

Introduction

෨

The Hebrew term for sacrifice, *korban*, has evolved to designate three different but related meanings. This phenomenon occurred in other languages as well. In its primary use, a sacrifice is a gift, an offering given from humans to God. It involves an object, usually an animal, which is transferred from the human to the divine realm. In its second use, which emerged later, the term refers to giving up a vital interest for a higher cause. Someone may sacrifice his property, comfort, limb, or even life for his children, country, or in order to fulfill an obligation. This latter sense of sacrifice also entails giving, but in this case it is giving *up* or *for*, and not giving *to*.

Owing to the lack of actual transfer, this second meaning of sacrifice does not appear in either biblical or rabbinic Hebrew, nor does it appear in Greek or Latin. While the phrase "x sacrificed to" is abundant in the early layer of Hebrew, the phrase "x sacrificed for," such as "x sacrificed his interest for," is absent altogether. The second use arose only in later layers of Hebrew and the European languages. Yet there is an inner logic to the extension of the term's use from the first sense to the second. Though no transfer has actually taken place in giving up individual interests for others or a country, the verb "to sacrifice for" can be construed indirectly as a giving of a gift by the individual to the nation or for the good of others.

The third meaning of *korban* is manifested by an intriguing development in its use in many languages. In Modern Hebrew, *korban* denotes not only an offering but also a victim of a crime; yet in biblical, rabbinic, and medieval Hebrew as well as in Greek and Latin, no such use exists. This additional use of the term "sacrifice", referring to both an offering and a crime victim, appeared in other languages such as Arabic, Spanish, and German before Hebrew. One of this book's concerns is to understand the depth of such an extension along with its implications for the complex relationship between sacrifice and violence.

This book is structured following the distinction between the first two senses of sacrifice: "sacrificing to" and "sacrificing for." Each use directs us to a different field of inquiry. "Sacrificing to" involves mainly the religious sphere. It engages such questions as ritual, substitution, atonement, and the ways in which different religious traditions developed complex alternatives to replace and yet replicate animal sacrifice as the main mode of worship. The study of sacrifice through this lens has received intense attention from different fields of investigation: the sociology of religion, psychoanalysis, anthropology, evolutionary biology, comparative religion, and cultural studies. My book draws inspiration from this immense body of literature, but I do not trace or map it in any systematic fashion. I refer to it selectively in line with the argument that I wish to pursue.

Though the historical and textual material for my examination of "sacrificing to" mainly focuses on biblical along with later Jewish and Christian developments, I aim to provide a larger theory of sacrifice and ritual as well as their relation to violence. My investigation does not follow the varied unfoldings of the notion of sacrifice in medieval Jewish mysticism and philosophy, or in modern Jewish thought. Needless to say, this book does not presume to cover the complex field of "sacrificing to" in different religions and traditions. Yet as an attempt to formulate a larger perspective on the subject, *On Sacrifice* strives to uncover a central feature of the phenomenon that will, I hope, resonate with other practices and traditions.

The distinction between a "gift" and an "offering" lies at the core of my effort to elucidate the meaning of the practice of sacrifice. Sacrifice is a specific kind of gift given within a hierarchical structure. The gap that is opened between the gift and the offering makes the possibility of rejection immanent in the practice of sacrifice. Exploring this distinction at the heart of "sacrificing to" will reveal two features that are essential to sacrifice: ritual and violence. Ritual and violence are opposing responses to the same anxiety of rejection. The nature of sacrifice as an offering will thus shed light on the central components of violence and ritual. Understanding sacrifice as an offering located within a hierarchical structure will also expose deep tensions that are embedded in the notion of sacrifice as an expression of love and practice of atonement. The rise of substitutes for sacrifice within the Christian and Jewish traditions from the first century onward will be discussed at the end of my consideration of "sacrificing to." The extremely diverse ways in which these traditions have shaped substitutes to sacrifice will highlight both the nature of sacrifice and the attempts in these traditions to overcome its inherent tensions.

The second part of this book, which is devoted to "sacrificing for," involves different realms altogether— the political and moral spheres. Self-sacrifice for another individual, value, or collective seems key to much of ethical life and political organization. In Kant's moral philosophy, as in other moral theories, the core of morality is the capacity to transcend the self along with its drives and interests, and therefore, as Kant formulated it, moral drama resides in the conflict between self-transcendence and self-love. While endorsing the value of self-transcendence, my study of the relationship between self-sacrifice and violence will try to show the way in which misguided self-transcendence has a potential to lead to far greater evils and harms than those that are motivated by excessive self-love. Unraveling the internal relationship between self-transcendence and violence will provide what I believe to be a preferable, deeper account of moral conflict.

War is a realm in which heroic self-sacrifice as well as utter violence and brutality are manifested. In my attempt to probe the relationship between self-transcendence and violence, I will try to demonstrate that the simultaneous occurrence of these two aspects of war is not accidental and that they are intrinsically connected. Focusing on "sacrificing for" will thus lead to investigating the role of sacrifice in war and the function of the state as a sacrificial bond.

The two parts of this essay—"sacrificing to" and "sacrificing for"—touch on two very different fields of inquiry that can stand independent of one another. Yet in following the ways in which various languages have extended the use from one realm to another, we might discover some shared deep structures that encompass rich and diverse realms of human life.

Sacrificing to

❧

Offering, Rejection, and Ritual

I

Sacrifice is the most primary and basic form of ritual. The elimination of animal sacrifice from contemporary Western religious life came about as a result of a cataclysmic moment. In Judaism, the ritual of sacrifice reached an abrupt end with the destruction of the temple in Jerusalem during the first century. The alternatives to temple worship that emerged out of this crisis within rabbinic culture, though "sublimating" temple sacrifice, were to a certain degree modeled after the sacrifice, and kept its ethos and drive. Christianity replaced all sacrifices with one ultimate sacrificial event: the sacrifice of the son of God. That sacrifice eclipsed all previous ones, making them redundant and void.[1] Hence Christianity did not do away with the idea of sacrifice; it founded itself on the supreme sacrifice, which within the Catholic tradition is reenacted in the church's ritual.

What is it about sacrifice that is so essential to human expression and life? I am not going to address this problem by investigating the origins of sacrifice. I doubt the explanatory power of such speculation, since it arbitrarily assumes that the moment of origin, if there is such a thing, has a privileged position regarding either the meaning of a phenomenon or its endurance.[2] I wish to initiate my investigation with a different sort of beginning, a literal one—the first account of sacrifice within the biblical narrative. An attentive reading of the first sacrifices offered at the emergence of humanity by Cain and Abel, and the bloodshed that resulted from this foundational sacrificial moment, has a lot to teach us concerning the meaning, trauma, and violence in sacrifice.

> Abel became a keeper of sheep, and Cain became a tiller of the soil. In the course of time, Cain brought an offering to the Lord from the fruit of the soil. And Abel, for his part, brought the choicest of the firstlings of his flock. The Lord paid heed to Abel and his offering, but to Cain and his offering He paid no heed. Cain was much distressed and his face fell. (Gen. 4:2–5)

The first biblical account of sacrifice has its source in spontaneous giving from the produce of each of the brothers to God. The story stresses the expectation of the giver that his sacrifice be accepted, and the utter devastation that results from its rejection. It seems that such anticipation aims at establishing a bond between the giver and receiver, in which the reception of the gift will establish the continuity of the flow of goods. The goal of the sacrifice is to produce a gift cycle. The tale postulates an essential connection between rejection and sacrifice; the risk of rejection is inherent in the act of sacrifice. Why Cain's offering was refused is a mystery, and the different explanations that have been proposed in the scholarly literature are inadequate. The text itself does not provide any substantive reason. This silence is significant; it is essential to this form of rejection that it remains inexplicable, as if nothing could be done to either predict or overcome it.

The privileging of Abel and dismissal of Cain seem to be as mysterious as human love and endearment. This unpredictable nature of love turns into a theme that haunts the entire book of Genesis. Why does Rebecca love Jacob and Isaac love Esau—an arbitrary division of love that ends up tragically defining the brothers' lives? And to what moral or other features can we attribute Jacob's preference—which will turn fatal—for Joseph over and above his brothers? The evasiveness of charm and capriciousness of attraction are at the root of much of the tragic dimension of the Genesis story. This entanglement has its starting point in my narrative in the privileging of one brother's sacrifice over the other's.

The inherent potential for rejection in the sacrificial act is manifested in the Hebrew term for the offering: *minchah*. In later priestly literature, this word was used to denote a subset of offerings—that is, vegetative offerings. Animal offerings were designated by the term *korban*. Yet Genesis doesn't distinguish between the two kinds of sacrifices. Abel's offering from his flock and

Cain's offering from his fruits are both called *minchah*. The term *minchah* is related to the verb *lehaniach*, which means to lay down or put before. The term *korban* is related to the verb *lekarev*, meaning to bring forward, approach, or move closer.[3]

Both of these words are used in contrast to the common term for a gift, *matanah*, a noun related to the verb *latet*, which means to give. While *matanah* signifies a gift that has been immediately transferred from giver to receiver, the term *minchah* or *korban*—as something that is brought forward or laid before—indicates that it is the receiver who will decide whether to take it or not. (The verb "to offer" as distinct from "to give" captures the nuance in English.) In the shift from *matanah* to *minchah*, from giving to bringing forward, a crucial gap is established between giving and receiving. In the case of Cain's sacrifice, this separation became rather momentous, inasmuch as it connects sacrifice with trauma.

An important linguistic phenomenon in the biblical material supplies the key to understanding sacrifice. In biblical language, gifts given between equals or from a superior to an inferior are always designated by the noun *matanah* and verb *latet*, implying that no gap between giving and receiving exists. The gift is an actual transfer to the beneficiary's domain. Only in the gifts offered from an inferior to a superior is the term *minchah* utilized, to stress the fact that the superior has the privilege of rejecting the gift. The giver, by bringing forward or laying down, is merely presenting something before the future beneficiary. His superior will take the next step, either to refuse or accept what was laid before him.

It is a mark of superiority that entry into the gift cycle is voluntary—an act of love rather than of duty. In his work on the gift, Marcel Mauss described the ethics of the gift as the obligation to receive and reciprocate.[4] This is true in a fraternal relation, but not among inferiors and superiors.[5] In the human-divine relationship, the divine privilege to reject is rooted in the fact that the sacrifice is actually an act of returning rather than giving. God is entitled, as the one who gave the produce in the first place, to refuse its return. The book of Deuteronomy articulates the expectation that pilgrims to the temple will bring a sacrifice: "And they shall not appear before God empty: every man shall give as he is able according to the blessing of God which he has given you" (Deut. 16:16–17). The one who brings a sacrifice gives to God what God has given to him. The sacrificial act is therefore a symbolic recycling of the gift to its origin.[6]

Two biblical vows, one by Jacob and another by Hannah, reflect the nature of an offering as the recycling of a gift and, through such recycling, the establishment of a gift cycle. When Jacob escaped from Esau, he pledged to make an offering if he returned home safely. The offering was formulated as follows: "And for all that You give me I will set aside a tithe for You" (Gen. 28:22). The tithe that Jacob vowed to offer to God is a return of a portion of what God would give him. Hannah's promise is far more dramatic and momentous. Hannah, who had been barren, made the following vow when praying for a child: "O Lord of Hosts, if You will look upon the suffering of Your maidservant and will remember me and not forget Your maidservant, and if You will grant Your maidservant a male child, I will dedicate him to the Lord for all the days of his life" (I Sam. 1:11). She later bore a child and named him Samuel—a name interpreted to signify that the child has been borrowed from God, and that Hannah fulfilled her vow, bringing the child to the temple to reside there all his life and serve God. On leaving him there, she declared to the priest: "It was this boy I prayed for; and the Lord has granted me what I asked of Him. I, in turn, thereby lend him to the Lord. For as long as he lives he is lent to the Lord" (I Sam. 1:27).

Unlike Jacob, who vowed to return only a tithe, a symbolic portion to express and acknowledge the gift, Hannah made a full return. She dedicated to God the child that God had given her. In the recycling of the gift, a gift cycle had been established. When Hannah came to the temple to visit Samuel, her child, Eli the priest blessed both her and Elkana, her husband: "'May the Lord grant you offspring by this woman in place of the loan she made to the Lord.' . . . For the Lord took note of Hannah; she conceived and bore three sons and two daughters" (I Sam. 2:20–21). God gave Samuel, who was offered back to God, and in turn he granted more children to the barren Hannah. A complete gift bond was effected.[7] Every offering is thus a return. The giver is permitted to use the rest of his property only after making the sacrificial gesture, which implies his gratitude and recognition that his goods are a gift of God.[8] Hence, the bringing of the first fruit to the temple allows the giver to consume the rest of the field for his purposes. He is just returning what he received, in the guise of giving.

The fact that the offering is given within such a hierarchical structure precludes the suspicion that it is a crude form of bribe or nourishment to God by the believer.[9] A middle-class person cannot bribe a billionaire; he can bribe another middle-class person who might be slightly better off than he is. The gift of sacrifice to God, who is in the first place the provider of the good and in no need of it, functions as a token of submission and gratitude, and its reception is not driven by need or interest but rather is an expression of welcoming and goodwill. *Sacrifice is thus a gift given within a hierarchical context in which the ordinary obligation to receive and return is not valid. As such, a cycle of gift exchange is not necessarily established with the presentation of the offering, and a dangerous gap between giving and receiving is opened up, creating a potential for rejection and trauma.*

The centrality of the gift expressed by the term *minchah*, which described the first offering, sheds light on the diverse functions of sacrifice as a whole. W. Robertson Smith, who laid the foundation for the study of sacrifice in the Bible, divided its function into three: communion, gift, and expiation. Communion, which according to Smith is the primordial and privileged function of sacrifice, is achieved through the shared consumption of the substance of the animal, thereby binding gods and humans with flesh-and-blood ties.[10] The more secondary function, the gift, serves its role of feeding the gods, and is based on later developed notions of property and its transfer. Expiation, the third function, is the role of the sacrifice as absolving, which developed, claims Smith, in the context of an overwhelming sense of guilt and sin.

Smith's division parallels the three forms of sacrifice as articulated in Leviticus: the peace offering (*shelamim*), in which portions of the sacrifice are given from the altar to the person who brings it for consumption, serves to create a communion with God; the burnt offering (*olah*), which is completely consumed on the altar, functions as a pure gift; and the sin offering (*chattat*) is the expiatory sacrifice. Smith saw in this list a final priestly editing of a long developmental process. His trajectory of the process from communion to expiation was based on Julius Wellhausen's work, which dated the priestly material as the last stratum in scripture.[11]

Regardless of the questionable accuracy of the chronological speculations, it appears that sacrifice within the biblical context is better understood through the gesture of the gift.[12] By way of the gift, communion can be divorced from the literal notion that God's altar and the offerer share the consumed animal. The acceptance of the sacrifice implies entry into the reciprocal gift cycle.[13] Solidarity is defined by the borders of the gift cycle, and it is through this exchange that communion transpires.[14]

Atonement, as I will discuss later, can also be achieved through the gift, which assumes a substitute giving of the self. The gift, within the biblical tradition, is not one of the functions of sacrifice; it is the central category of sacrifice, but its meaning as a gift varies and is multilayered.[15] In its essence as an offering as opposed to a gift, the sacrifice defies the common ethics of giving since its acceptance is not secured.

The fatal possibility of rejection gives rise to an important function of "ritual": successful transfer. Ritual is a prescribed procedure meant to guarantee the transfer's success. Adherence to detailed routine makes the passage from laying down to acceptance less fraught. *Ritual is thus a protocol that protects from the risk of rejection.* In that respect, ritual is analogous to legal systems as a whole insofar as they impose order while confronting the unreliability and capriciousness of emotional responses. It makes cooperation and the division of labor independent of the chaos of personal encounter; it is therefore an attempt to project a stable future.[16]

The ritual's intricate rules serve as a shield for the human approaching God. Any change in the protocol might be lethal, like walking in a minefield. This shield comes at the expense of visibility. The one who is offering a sacrifice wishes to appear before God, to be made visible and join the gift cycle. And yet being in the spotlight before power can be terrifying. As in sending a complaint to the tax authorities, files might be opened, and the results are uncertain. In a negative assessment of the presumed piety expressed in vowing, the Talmud states: "Whoever initiates a vow his record is examined" (Jerusalem Talmud, Nedarim 1:1, 36:4). Vowing as a voluntary act of accepting an obligation (a demand beyond the norm) draws dangerous attention.[17] It is no wonder that Job's fall began the moment he was noticed, owing to God's remark to Satan: "Have you noticed my servant Job? There is no one like him in all the earth" (Job 1:8). In his horror of visibility, Job yearns for anonymity and admonishes God for acting as humanity's guardian: "Am I the sea or the Dragon that You have set a watch over me? . . . What is man, that You make much of him, that You fix Your attention upon him? You inspect him every minute. Will You not look away from me for a while, Let me be, till I swallow my spittle? If I have sinned, what have I done to You watcher of men? Why make of me Your target, and a burden to myself?" (Job 7:12–17).

Ritual as a protocol for an approach erases the individuation of the one who is approaching. Such a person is one among many who follow the routine, approaching under the canopy of the secure and recognizable. The acceptance of such a gift is not unique, but at least it is safe. It secures enough attention without drawing too much of it. It is a sign of religious intimacy that the pious test the borders of ritual, and hence approach without following the protocol. It is a mark of their religious standing that they appear before God without following the

strict procedure of entry. "Love undermines the order":
with intimacy, playfulness serves as a substitute for the
protocol of access. Yet a wrongly presumed intimacy, as
in the case of Aaron's sons Nadav and Avihu, might be
fatal. The brothers spontaneously brought forth an alien
fire that was not commanded by God and were immediately put to death.

In the spontaneous sacrifice offered by Cain and Abel
at humanity's emergence, before there was any protocol,
death resulted from the gift's rejection. In the priestly
material, though, the relationship between death and
sacrifice is reversed. Nadav's and Avihu's deaths as a piv-
otal moment in establishing detailed ritual came about
because of their attempt to act outside the protocol:
"Now Aaron's sons Nadav and Avihu each took his fire
pan, put fire in it, and laid incense on it; they offered
before the Lord alien fire, which he had not enjoined
upon them. And fire came forth from the Lord and consumed them; thus they died at the instance of the Lord"
(Lev. 10:1–2). Their presumed attempt at offering occurred right after the initiation of the priests by Moses,
and consecration of the tabernacle at the inauguration
of the priestly ritual. Given this, the death of both signifies the protocol's power and price of deviating from
it after it has been established. It is no wonder that the
most detailed rituals recorded in the priestly material—
prescribing the way in which the high priest can safely
approach the temple's inner sanctum—were introduced

with reference to these traumatic deaths: "The Lord spoke to Moses after the death of the two sons of Aaron who died when they drew too close to the presence of the Lord. The Lord said to Moses: Tell your brother Aaron that he is not to come at will into the shrine behind the curtain. In front of the cover that is upon the ark lest he dies; for I appear in the cloud over the cover. Thus only shall Aaron enter the shrine" (Lev. 16:1–2). The establishment of ritual as an effort to overcome the anxiety of rejection shifts the locus of danger from the gift's refusal to false intimacy.

Ritual is an attempt to grapple with the inherent unpredictability of rejection. In order to smooth the passage from bringing forward to acceptance, practitioners tend to go a step further and endow ritual with magical powers. The magical reading of ritual introduces a causal dimension that closes the gap between giving and receiving, thereby ensuring acceptance of the gift and leaving nothing voluntary to the recipient. In that respect, the magical reading is the extreme opposite of intimacy. When the protocol is endowed with causal power, all personal elements are erased from the approach. We can imagine how shattering the prophetic corrective to such an urge was, when the prophets proclaimed that the whole structure of ritual—its daily forms, calendar, and detailed protocol—could turn abhorrent to the recipient—a burden that God might detest.[18] Causation cannot replace desire.

II

René Girard, who has investigated the nexus of sacrifice
and violence, contends that violence has an accelerating,
uncontrolled nature. It escalates through sequels of re-
taliatory events. The aim of an animal or human sacrifice
is to halt the unbridled spread of violence. Sacrifice thus
serves a vital purification role. The violence performed
on the sacrificial victim releases a violent anger on a target that is close to the actual subject of violence and yet
far from tied to it. Thus one side is satisfied while the
other side is not moved to retaliate.[19] It is crucial, according to Girard, to choose a proper victim—one both
near and far away enough to serve as a scapegoat. The
failure to calibrate this may cause a sacrificial crisis. If
the victim is too distant from the actual subject, it is use-
less to shift the rage. If the victim is too close, the subject
will retaliate, and the sacrificial violence will not stop
the cycle but rather contribute to its spread.

A proper understanding of Cain's and Abel's sacrifices
provides an alternative to Girard's account concerning
the nexus between violence and sacrifice. The source of
violence is in the rejection from the sacrificial bond, the
exclusion from the gift cycle. Because Cain's gift was refused, he was excluded from the most meaningful bond.
He brought forward his gift, thus showing his desire to
take part, and was slapped in the face, annihilated. It is
far worse to have one's gift rejected than to fail to receive

a gift. When someone receives a gift while another person does not, the latter person is excluded from a cycle to which he did not display any initial desire to belong. The rejection of a gift, on the other hand, is a harsher form of exclusion. It is an utter dismissal, not only a form of ignoring. Cain asserted his presence through an act of violence. He destroyed the bond that he was excluded from and then made his weight felt again. The response to rejection from the cycle of bounty, to marginalization from what constitutes being itself, might be the deepest element in violence. The first murder was not only motivated by jealousy; it came from an acute response to banishment and isolation. *The exclusion from the possibility of giving is a deeper source of violence than the deprivation that results from not getting.*

Forced barrenness stands at the source of violence. The exclusion of a person from the cycle of giving is a thorough humiliation. It diminishes him from the effectiveness of giving and weight of contributing.[20] Assigning a person exclusively to the receiving end dooms him to passive receptivity and dependency, depriving him of the expression of love. When a child does not reciprocate his parent's love, the parent is less devastated than if the child refuses to receive his gift and rejects altogether the goods that the parent wishes to bestow on him. Because the capacity to give is so profoundly human, its denial might turn into violence.

It is no wonder, then, that the liturgical and scriptural language surrounding the sacrifice is loaded with references to hopes and promises of desire.[21] The other side of the dark fear of rejection is the expectation that the gift will be pleasing and desirable. As a testimony to this fear, sacrifices can become like gifts that not only are unreciprocated but also merely accumulate and become a burden, or like letters that are not only ignored but never opened as well. Each of these gifts and letters is another proof of the giver's annihilation.

Cain's punishment was proper and accurate, a kind of perfect retribution. He was not executed but rather excluded forever. He was cast away, forced to wander: "Cain left the presence of the Lord and settled in the land of Nod, east of Eden" (Gen. 4:16). His initial sacrifice from the fruits that he grew was meant to ensure the continuation of that bounty; he wished to return the fruits he was given in order to get more of them, thereby fueling that crucial process. Cain was punished: "If you till the soil, it shall no longer yield its strength to you. You shall become a ceaseless wanderer on earth" (Gen. 4:12). The land—Cain's source of bounty and life—will turn barren.

Instead of approaching God with another sacrifice, Cain killed his brother. This time, the entity on the receiving end is the earth that took in the brother's blood: "Therefore you shall be cursed from the earth, which opened its mouth to receive your brother's blood from your hand" (Gen. 4:11).[22] There will be no return from what might be described as a perverse blood gift; barrenness and wandering are the only outcomes of a futile attempt at asserting presence. The land that covered the blood will cover itself from the murderer; it will no longer open its treasures and fertility to Cain.

An attentive analysis of the terms designating sacrifice—*minchah* and *korban*—unlocks the meaning of the practice of sacrifice as an offering brought before God and aimed at establishing the bond of the gift cycle. Given within a hierarchical structure, sacrifice is an offering as opposed to a gift, thus opening a possible gap between giving and receiving. The trauma of rejection and its violent outcome is at the root of ritual as a protocol of approach that attempts to bridge the abyss of offering. Why is rejection inherent in approach? A more nuanced look at the problem will reveal another relationship between violence and sacrifice, this time in the form of the trial: the relationship between sacrifice and love.

Sacrifice, Exchange, and Love

I

Love is a noninstrumental relationship outside of what appears to be the sphere of exchange. The other is loved for his own sake, for what he is, rather than for what can be derived from him. The mark of love as noninstrumental is attentiveness. Lust or contract, love's rivals, are not attentive to the other; their focus is on satisfaction and interest. Attentiveness as a form of affirmation is what makes love so precious.

Love is a difficult task within relationships of power asymmetry and total dependency. God wishes to be loved, not only feared or admired—a nearly impossible quest, given the total dependency of humans on him. With such dependency, the human temptation to form an instrumental relationship to God will always lurk in the background. Can someone love a person on whom his fate and that of his loved ones are dependent? The tendency to instrumentalize is in fact immanent in the nature of this great asymmetry of power. Given this, God suffers from the rich-spouse predicament: he can never be sure that he is not loved for his money, or to put it more bluntly, he will always be in doubt as to whether he is loved altogether.

In the Job narrative, this divine self-doubt is what made God so vulnerable to Satan's seduction. When God praised Job to Satan, he was actually inviting Satan's challenge: Maybe Job's loyalty is all about the goods that you bestowed on him? Take away the goods and let us see what happens. The poisonous drops that Satan spilled were effective. He was granted permission to embark on the road of tormenting Job, because he echoed a deep-seated inner doubt. Trial has its roots in the quest for love's proof within an asymmetrical relationship of dependency and power.

Suffering and withdrawal can be one unfortunate way out of this dilemma of love, but there is another, more awful path. Given the noninstrumental nature of love, sacrificing for the sake of someone is a mark of love. Yet assuming the dependency on God, is a genuine sacrifice possible here? What sort of offering can be brought to God—a gift that will not be considered part of the exchange relationship? With the Almighty, who can always reciprocate something greater and better, as the addressee of such an offering, any offering to him might as well become a piece of the economy of exchange rather then an expression of love. The other foundational narrative of sacrifice in Genesis—the binding of Isaac—refers to such a gift outside the realm of exchange.

All sacrifices might be a form of exchange—offerings to ensure the gift cycle—and yet sacrificing a son could not serve that purpose. Someone might sacrifice all his property, but based on a calculated expectation of getting a greater share in return. A person might sacrifice all that he has and in turn receive more. This isn't the case with the sacrifice of a son. For Abraham, nothing could compensate for his son's loss, since a child has ultimate value. God, in his trial of Abraham, wished to ascertain that Abraham didn't worship him simply because he had given him a son at such an old age. He tested that premise by demanding that Abraham sacrifice his Isaac. In this way, the same anxiety of instrumentality gave birth to this horrifying request. The urge to bestow is essential to love, but the loving partner wants that bestowing to be *part* of the relationship and not the *reason* for it. The trial's purpose is supposed to guarantee giving as part of the relationship, rather than serve as a rationale for it. The gift will be haunted by this imbalance, especially within an asymmetrical structure of power.

When Abraham showed his willingness to offer something that could never be reciprocated, God renounced his desire for the gift's actualization. God, who promised Abraham descendants and life, commanded him not to touch the child. Abraham instead sacrifices a substitute for Isaac: a ram, caught in the bushes. This act establishes another meaning to the exchange implied in the sacrifice. The animal sacrifice is a symbolic replacement for self-sacrifice, or the sacrifice of a son.[23] In its place as a foundational narrative of the sacrifice, the binding of Isaac outlines the meaning of the sacrificial gesture: *the sacrifice that as a gift seems to be part of an exchange cycle, is actually a symbol for a gift that cannot be reciprocated.* This substitution allows the operation of the gift cycle. God will respond to such sacrifice since it ensures symbolically that his bestowing is part of the relationship rather than the reason for it.

The role of sacrifice as a substitute might be connected to another attempt to distinguish a gift exchange from a market one. This distinction involves the different form in which the duty of reciprocity is viewed in these practices. In the market, the receiver is legally bound to reciprocate; with the gift, reciprocity is only a moral duty. If it were a legal duty for a person to reciprocate a gift, a duty that can be enforced by law, this would taint the act of giving, turning it into something driven by an instrumental calculation in the first place. The divide between the legal and moral duty for a receiver to reciprocate is anchored in the fact that in gift exchange, giving is considered a part of the relationship, not the justification for it. In the market, the exchange is the rationale for the encounter, not its expression. In the gift cycle, therefore, a lack of reciprocity on the receiver's part doesn't serve as a legal reason for a claim to return the gift or demand reciprocity. It might be cause for a more severe reaction, with the receiver opting out of the relationship altogether, since he views it as exploitative and asymmetrical. The giver whose gift was not reciprocated might feel that he had been betrayed as well as fooled into believing there was a relationship apart from the giving.

In order to underscore the distinction more clearly, let me draw attention to the microstructures of gift giving. Imagine that a guest comes to a dinner party bearing the gift of a sum of money equivalent to the giver's estimation of the cost of his meal. The host would most likely be offended by this gift, because it would turn the occasion of a friendly dinner party into an instance of market exchange. A more socially acceptable gift here would be something that served as a substitute, a kind of token for the guest's appreciation of the host's kindness as well as a sign of the guest's future intention to reciprocate. The gifts that families of patients present to hospital staff are made in a similar spirit. These gifts are regarded not as a form of compensation for the nurses' and orderlies' work but rather as an expression of gratitude for the patient care they provided. Such tokens have no place in a market exchange, in which the purchaser of a commodity must offer up more than a sign of thanks. The sacrifice, on the contrary, ought to exemplify just such a sign, and if it does, it is marked as belonging to the domain of gratitude and love expression instead of the very different sphere of the market economy.

This line of reasoning allows us to understand why the giving of cash can be perceived as an insult versus a tribute. In bringing an object rather than cash to a dinner party or any analogous occasion, the giver expresses her attentiveness to the recipient's tastes, which is the ultimate mark of care. The best gift, moreover, is something superfluous—that is, something that the recipient wouldn't necessarily have bought for herself with her own resources. (For this reason, it would be strange to bring a bag of groceries as a gift.) Yet the gift's redundancy is always in danger of deteriorating to a functional exchange.

The line between gifts and commodities is never firm and sometimes blurs, leading some theorists of the gift to regard gift giving as a form of market exchange. Pierre Bourdieu offers one description of the gift cycle:

> Gift exchange is an exchange in and by which the agents strive to conceal the objective truth of the exchange, i.e. the calculation which guarantees the equity of the exchange. If "fair exchange," the direct swapping of equiv-

alent values, is the truth of gift exchange, gift exchange
is a swapping which cannot acknowledge itself as such.[24]

This is a mistaken reading, I would argue, since gifts
function as ritual symbols that aim at solidifying and expressing a variety of relationships.[25] The gift certificate,
exchange slip, and bridal Web sites for retail department
stores posting engaged couples' lists of desired household
objects before weddings are all examples of such blur-
ring. All are attempts to impose indirect market efficiency
on a practice that rests fundamentally on redundancy.
Yet even in such cases of market intrusion, efforts to
avoid cash payments and approximate superfluousness
still preserve a semblance of gift giving. (Of course, cash
giving is not unheard of, but it is most common when
the relationship between the giver and recipient is primary and close. A close relative such as a brother or
an uncle may write a check as a wedding gift, since the
solidity of the relationship isn't in question.)

The three sacrificial acts examined thus far—Cain and
Abel, the sacrifice brought by Aaron's sons Nadav and
Avihu along with their deaths, and the binding of Isaac,
or the *akedah*—attest to the complexities of sacrifice as
an offering and the possibility of rejection inherent in
the act; the function of ritual as a protocol presumed to
overcome the anxiety of rejection, and the subsequent
lethal price of any attempt to divert from this protocol
via false intimacy; and the inherent fragility of sacrifice
as a gift, given its potential to degrade into a mere mar-

ket exchange owing to the asymmetry of power, and the subsequent trial of love that springs out of that tension.

The particular concerns that arise from each of these constitutive moments also depend on an underlying diversity, assumed by each of them, in the image of God. In Cain's and Abel's offerings, God appears as an inscrutable sovereign whose love and rejection is delegated mysteriously. In the *akedah*, he emerges as "the rich husband," a tormented, dependent personality who is needy precisely because of his metaphysical superiority. Finally, with the development of the priestly protocol, God is an all-powerful being approached by procedurally agreed-on forms. This variety of images defining the different aspects of the offering doesn't pose a contradiction but rather, when put together, attests to the multifaceted nature of the divine being as experienced in the biblical tradition.[26]

II

In establishing a connection between sacrifice and substitute, I can now point to a central feature of sacrifice: atonement. Atonement is a procedure through which the initially deserved retributive punishment is revoked based on the fact that the punishment can be transposed to the symbolic realm. The symbolization of the punishment can be achieved by two means: directing the punishment to a representation of the subject (such as the sacrificial animal), or replacing the punishment itself with a lesser symbolic pain administered on the same subject.

Scholars of biblical sacrificial ritual have identified two functions of the sacrificial blood that are key to atonement (*kaparah*) in the biblical tradition. The first is that of cleansing. The Hebrew verb *le-khaper* stems from the Akkadian *kuppuru*, which means to clean, to purify. The sin, which takes on an ontological quality, accumulates in the midst of the community and causes the withdrawal of God's presence from the temple. The sacrificial ritual, and in particular the Yom Kippur one, is a cleansing of sin from the temple, ensuring the return of God's protective presence. The blood of the sacrifice, when sprinkled on the altar, serves as a cleansing agent, purifying the temple from the stain of sin.[27]

The second function of the sacrificial blood, connected to the second meaning of *kaparah*, is that of ransom. In the book of Numbers, God forbids people from accepting "a ransom (*kofer*) for the life of a murderer who is guilty of capital crime; he must be put to death" (Num. 35:31). Another ransom reference occurs in the book of Leviticus in the prohibition against drinking blood: "For the life of the flesh is in the blood, and I have assigned it to you for making expiation for your lives upon the altar; it is the blood, as life, that effects expiation" (Lev. 17:11). As Rashi notes in his commentary on this passage, blood as a representation of life can serve as a ransom—that is, a symbolic substitute for the sacrificer's life.[28]

If the sacrifice is to work in this second sense, as a symbolic substitute, it is essential that the one who brings the sacrifice designate it as a substitute. The presenter thereby creates a representational relationship between himself and the sacrifice. This relationship is implied in the act preceding the sacrifice's offering, as in this passage: "He shall lay his hand upon the head of the burnt offering, that it may be acceptable in his behalf, in expiation for him" (Lev. 1:5). In this gesture, the gift and expiation are mingled. Atonement is achieved through the symbolic substitute of the self. Alternatively, ritual expiation might involve yet another procedure in which a victim is not brought to the altar but rather sent away, as the one who carries the sin. In such a case, the animal is not a symbolic representation; it is a vehicle for projection:

> Aaron shall lay both his hands upon the head of the live goat and confess over it all the iniquities and transgressions of the Israelites, whatever their sins, putting them on the head of the goat; and it shall be sent off to the wilderness through a designated man. Thus the goat shall carry on it all their iniquities to an inaccessible region; and the goat shall be set free in the wilderness. (Lev. 17:21–22)

When Aaron holds the goat, and combines that with the speech act of confession, he transfers the burden of sin to the animal, which then carries it away. Confession in its most primary sense is not an act of disclosure or admission; it alleviates the burden and passes it on. This sense of confession has been preserved to this day, even in secular contexts such as psychotherapy that are bereft of the assumption of the ontology of sin being passed from one subject to another. Confession is often experienced as an act of letting go, or liberating the self from a hidden burden. And yet the contemporary therapeutic context still retains the idea of transference, if only as a metaphor when the secret's burden is passed on to a shared carrier—as if the weight of secrecy is greater than the possible shame of disclosure.

The substitution characteristic of sacrifice in its biblical sense is also an attempt on the offerer's part to deflect violence away from him toward the sacrificial object or being. The offerer is thus motivated by fear and anxiety (rather than, as Girard suggests, anger). He does not postulate the sacrifice as a substitute for venting his anger and rage, thereby satisfying his desire for revenge without opening a new cycle of violence, as understood by Girard. Instead, the sacrifice is a substitute for the violence that the offerer himself might deserve. This function gives rise to a second kind of anxiety, which is an outcome of the sacrificial logic. Previously I examined the offerer's fear of rejection; substitution raises another worry. This anxiety is predicated on a firm sense of one's own guilt or criminality—that one has done wrong; that some act of violence must occur in retribution; and that one's proposed substitute—the victim or scapegoat on which one hopes the violence will be directed—is basically innocent. Criminals themselves cannot become sacrificial victims. The victim's innocence is what makes him capable of becoming a vehicle for ultimate projection. For this reason, the biblical rules guiding the choice of the sacrificial victim prescribe that one find an innocent, unblemished creature. A crime against an innocent substitute has to occur in order to allow for atonement.

The innocence of the sacrificed subject is at the root of an important linguistic development in the term *korban* in Hebrew and other languages. In Modern Hebrew, *korban* designates not only a sacrifice but also a crime victim. The media and law, for instance, both describe rape victim as *korban ones*. In biblical, rabbinic, and medieval Hebrew, by contrast, no such use exists. *Korban* only means an "offering."

The idea of sacrifice was first expanded to include crime victims as well as offerings in languages other than Hebrew. The Arabic term *adcha* indicates a sacrifice to God as well as a crime victim (*dachiya*), and the German term *opfer* and the Spanish word *victima* are further examples along these lines, as is the word "victim" in English, which according to *Webster's Third New International Dictionary* means "a living being sacrificed to some deity in the performance of religious act" (in religious usage), or "put to death, tortured or mulcted by another." In both the Hebrew and Latin, the primary meaning of "victim" was an offering to God, and it was extended to include victims of crime. Although the contemporary use in the first sense—as a sacrifice—is now rare, this was not always so. In Latin, the extension never occurred, and the term *victima* is solely used for an offering to the gods and not for crime victims. The same is true of Greek, which uses different words to designate an offering and a crime victim. The essential commonality between the two senses, and perhaps the source of the extension from the primary to the secondary meaning, is undeniably the victim's innocence. The one who is attacked and violated is as innocent as the object offered to the gods.[29] A criminal killed in a gang war will not be portrayed as *korban*, or a victim, since he lacks innocence.

The expansion of the term from sacrifice as an offering to the description of crime victims is not only a linguistic phenomenon; it coincided with the development of the Christian tradition. Jesus was simultaneously an innocent victim of a crime, put to death for no justified reason by Jews and Romans, and the ultimate atoning sacrifice.[30] The foundational narrative of the sacrifice in Christianity, in other words, merges the crime victim and the sacrifice into the same persona. Why is this so? I would suggest that this came about in an attempt to overcome the inherent tension in the substitution idea.

This point needs further explanation. As we have seen, in order to serve as a substitute, the sacrifice has to be innocent. The necessary innocence of the sacrifice creates an inherent crime in any sacrifice; the atoned party achieves atonement through an innocent substitute. The act of atonement seems to need atonement in itself.[31]

When a human being—such as Jesus—is the substitute, tension escalates, and indeed in certain trends within the Christian doctrine, the people blamed for Jesus's death are those he atoned for, since he died because of their sins.[32] The claim that a different party, rather than those who achieved atonement, performed the killing, may in an improper fashion defuse such difficult stress. Whereas Jews and/or Romans executed Jesus, those who had been expiated by his sacrifice constitute another group—one that remained faithful to his mission, and mourned and resisted his death. The Jews and/or Romans, we might say, committed the crime whose collateral benefit was the atonement of the faithful.

Jesus had to be both a victim and a sacrifice. Had he been a "pure" offering instead—without having suffered victimization at the hands of his Jewish and Roman betrayers and tormentors—the atoned party would have been in an intolerable situation. This group would have made amends through its own murderous act. The solution was to introduce a third party as the guilty, criminal element responsible and blamed for the crime. Thus, the desire to avoid violence toward the innocent substitute leads the atoned party—the party of the faithful—to construct and blame a guilty party for the victim's killing. The guilty group, tragically, will serve repeatedly in the history of Christianity as a future target of Christian-generated violence.

The presumed guilty ones—at first understood as Jews and Romans, but over time, seen as the Jews alone—

will remain associated with and a target of violence, since without such violence and blame the sacrifice itself is tainted. This logic forces the emergence of a double scapegoat: first, Jesus, who is the innocent carrier for the community's sin, and second, the Jews, who designated the former to be the scapegoat. Anti-Semitism serves as a mechanism to absolve the troubling guilt stemming from the necessary innocence of the sacrificial victim.

Within their own history of thought and practice, however, Christians have dealt with the paradox of innocence in a theologically far deeper and richer way—involving a reversal of the offering. God himself offered his son for everyone's sake. The New Testament and patristic literature has depicted Jesus by using a variety of sacrificial analogies—the Pascal lamb, the scapegoat, the *tamid* (the daily sacrifice), Isaac to God's Abraham in a replay of the *akedah*, and the high priest sacrificing himself instead of the sacrifice. If there is a problem with the sacrificial victim's innocence, it is a problem of the God who offered him, rather than of the atoned party that accepted the offering.

This reversal represents not only a resolution of the issue of innocence; it is also an upheaval in the offering's basic structure. Recall that the very concept of an offering as distinct from a gift entails the traumatic possibility of rejection. Ritual is the attempt to bridge the traumatic gap between giving and receiving. Since it is God who initiated the offering of his son—thereby reversing the hierarchy of giving through an act of love—there is no chance of refusal. Such a dramatic moment challenges the need for ritual. It is therefore understandable that within Pauline thinking, ritual was abolished once and for all when God assumed the offerer's side.[33] Yet not only was ritual challenged; the very concept of sacrifice had been eclipsed too. In this ultimate offering, the notion of the substitute is annulled, because there is no ram to replace the son (as was the case with Isaac). The offering of the son represented a nonexchangeable gift, given without a token. As such, it announced the sole exclusive sacrifice by becoming the ultimate substitute of all substitution.

During the same period in which this Christian notion of the end of sacrifice came about through the crucifixion, another system of substitution developed in rabbinic thinking as a result of the temple's destruction in Jerusalem. This system took a completely different direction, yet in structuring its own version of substitution to sacrifice, it uncovered the essential features of sacrifice. The analysis of this approach will be the subject of the next chapter.

Sacrifice and Its Substitutes

The issues raised thus far concerning sacrifice, its anxieties and trauma, and its relationship to ritual and violence can be made clearer as well as deeper by examining how the sacrificial system itself was replaced in Jewish life after the temple's destruction. This monumental religious crisis turned into a moment of opportunity. The rabbis devised alternatives to the sacrificial functions in ways that struggle and deal with the fears and stress inherent in sacrifice. Here, I wish to highlight three alternate elements—charity, suffering, and prayer.

Charity

The following story is recounted in rabbinic literature (Avot de-Rabbi Natan, version 1, chapter 4):

> Once Rabban Yochanan ben Zakai was exiting Jerusalem and Rabbi Yehoshua was following him. He saw the Temple destroyed. Rabbi Yehoshua said woe to us that the temple is destroyed—a place that the sins of Israel were atoned. He told him: my son, don't be in sorrow, we have one atonement equal to it. It is charity, since it said: "I desired charity not sacrifice." (Hosea 6:6)

It is not by chance that this statement is attributed to Rabban Yochanan ben Zakai, considered the main figure responsible for shaping Jewish life after the crisis of the destruction. The atoning power of charity can be understood in a simple manner. Giving to the poor and needy appeases God no less than does sacrifice; charity is therefore an act that atones.

In another rabbinic text (Babylonian Talmud, Baba Batra 10a), the nature of charity as an alternative sacrifice gains a deeper meaning:

R. Dusthai b. Yannai taught: Come and see how the manner of the Holy One, blessed be He, is not as the manner of human beings. When a human being brings a present to the king, there is a doubt whether it will be accepted or not; and if it be accepted, whether he will see the king. But the Holy One, blessed be He, is not so; if a man gives a coin to a poor man, he is rewarded and experiences the appearance of the Shekhinah; as it is written [Ps. 17:15]: "As for me, in *zedek* (charity) shall I behold thy face." R. Elazar used to give a coin to a poor man before praying, quoting the above verse. (ibid.)

The Talmudic statement sets charity within the problematic character of an offering. The acceptance of a gift presented to a king is never secure. If the gift is received and accepted, this is not necessarily a sign of the king embracing the one who brought it; it might be strictly exploitative. The giver of charity, on the other hand, is immune from the possibility of rejection; God will reveal himself to him.

In the next statement, the Talmud provides a bold reason for why charity secures this closing of the gap established by the gesture of the offering. This teaching is introduced by a rare formula: "Were it not written in Scripture one would not dare to say it." The phrase expresses the idea that the statement about to come is so daring that if it wasn't explicitly written in scripture, the interpreter would have not dared to say it:

R. Johanan said: What is the meaning of the verse, "he that has pity on the poor lends to God"? Were it not written in Scripture, one would not dare to say it: as it were, the borrower is a slave to the lender."

The logic of this reading works as follows: God is actually the one who is obligated to provide for the poor. The destitute are his creatures, whom he brought into the world. When a person provides charity to the poor, he is in fact paying God's debt. Charity is, therefore, like lending to God. The charity giver, by paying God's debt, transforms his relationship to God from a debtor to a lender. In that act of giving, the giver reverses the relationship of dependence between himself and God, since the one who owes is considered a slave to the lender. Charity is thus described as enslaving God, shifting his position from a creditor to a debtor.[34]

This reversal relates to the trauma of sacrifice in a complex fashion. As was explained above, sacrifice—*korban*—assumes that a person offers up a gift that might be rejected. It maintains an essential, hierarchical gap between giving and receiving. But in giving to the poor, no such gap exists. The poor person stretching forth his hand is not typically in a position to exercise his power of refusal; he must keep his hand outstretched to accept the offer of assistance. Since God is the one who has to feed the poor, however, the hand of the poor stands for God's hand. Charity is an actual gift to God that he couldn't refuse, because it is mediated through the hand of the desperate. A person binds God—his superior—to the gift cycle precisely by giving to a dependent—the poor.

This Talmudic position doesn't aim at providing an incentive for charity; if this were the case, the poor might become a mere instrument in "forcing" God into a debtor status. The statement rather provides a description of what actually happens in giving; it doesn't prescribe the aim of giving or the motivation for it. When someone gives out of compassion for the plight of the poor, he is entering a gift cycle that reverses the structure of the offering. *Charity is preferred over sacrifice because it erases the abyss between giving and receiving without recourse to ritual, which minimizes individuation. What is more, this way of giving reverses the hierarchical order implied in the offering of a sacrifice; charity reverses God's position from a lender to a borrower.*

Suffering

The Midrash, quoting a second-century source, designates affliction as a preferable alternative to sacrifice:

> R. Nehemeiah says: precious are chastisements. For just as sacrifices are the means of atonement, so also chastisements. What does it say about sacrifices? "And it shall be accepted for him to make atonement" [Lev. 1:4]. And what does it say in connection with chastisements? "And they shall be paid the punishment of their iniquity" [Lev. 26:43]. And not only this, but chastisements

atone even more than sacrifices. For sacrifices affect only one's money, while chastisements affect the body. And thus it says: "Skin for skin, yea all that a man hath will he give for his life." [Job 2:4][35]

When suffering is not mere retribution but instead serves as atonement, it is a different kind of substitute for animal sacrifice. Whereas sacrifice is a symbolic substitute for the punishment-deserving subject, suffering is a symbolic substitute for the punishment itself. The sinner is absolved because he has endured some suffering, although less than he deserves under a retributive scheme. This shift in the locus of substitution alters the substitute's status of innocence. The animal that is brought to a sacrificial altar must be both whole and innocent, or else it will be unable to perform its role.

By contrast, when pain is designated as the symbolic carrier for the punishment, the need for the subject's innocence and wholeness disappears, and is actually reversed. This theme is developed in the Midrashic reading of a verse from the fifty-first Psalm: "The sacrifices of God are a broken spirit; a broken and contrite heart" (Ps. 51:19).

R. Abba bar Yudan said: What God regards as unfit for sacrifice in an animal, He holds fit in a human being. In an animal, He regards as unfit one that is blind, or broken, or maimed or having a wen [Lev. 22:22]; but in a human being He holds a broken and contrite heart [Ps. 51:19] to be fit for an offering to Him.[36]

The subject who offers part of himself is bringing the broken self before God, in contrast to the sacrificial animal's innocence and wholeness.

A more detailed text concerning suffering and atonement is cited several times in rabbinic literature in the name of Rabbi Ishmael:

> Rabbi Ishmael says, there are four kinds of atonement. If one violated a positive commandment but repented, he hardly moves from his place before they forgive him. . . . If he has violated a negative commandment but repented, repentance suspends the punishment, and the Day of Atonement effects atonement. . . . If he has violated [a rule for which the punishment is] extirpation or death at the hands of an earthly court, but repented, repentance and the Day of Atonement suspend [the punishment] and suffering of the rest of days of the year will wipe away [the sin]. . . . But he through whom the Name of Heaven is profaned deliberately but who repented—repentance does not have power to suspend the punishment nor the Day of Atonement to atone, but repentance and the Day of Atonement atone for a third, suffering atones for a third, and death wipes away the sin, with suffering. (Tosefta Yoma 4:7–8)

This list provides a better understanding of the nature of the symbolic substitute postulated by suffering. Rabbi Ishmael's statement establishes atonement for the whole spectrum of sins without either the presence of the temple or functioning courts able to deliver punishment.

Jews were denied the use of these two institutions of atonement after the temple's destruction. The rabbi's list is therefore of immense importance in defining the alternative to sacrifice.

According to Rabbi Ishmael, repentance is a necessary condition for atonement for all sins from the light to the grave. In the case of someone transgressing a positive commandment for which no punishment is prescribed, repentance by itself is sufficient. When it comes to sins for which the sinner should have been punished, the following pattern emerges. Atonement is completed by an element of suffering that is less than the actual punishment designated in scripture for the sin. Such an element of symbolic suffering as substitute must be done in conjunction with repentance. In the second category mentioned by Rabbi Ishmael, the minor suffering from the fasting of Yom Kippur atones for transgressions of negative commandments that regularly would have been punished with lashes. In the third category, sins for which the punishment is death or execution are atoned for by repentance, fasting on Yom Kippur, and suffering that happens to a person throughout the year. Hence in the second and third categories, suffering serves as a symbolic substitute for a far harsher punishment. These two categories take on the role of sacrifice, symbolizing not the sinner but rather the punishment.

From the rabbinic perspective, the punishment set by the court is aimed at atonement. The punishment of lashes saves the sinner from death, *karet*, and the punishment of execution absolves the sinner, transforming him and thus making him eligible for the world to come.[37] Rabbi Ishmael, who was responding to the Jews' loss of privilege to judge and punish after the destruction, supplied a concept of atonement not only for a world without a temple but also for one without a court that punishes. The suffering of fasting on Yom Kippur becomes a stand-in for the lashes, and the suffering during the rest of the year becomes a substitute for execution. The pains that serve as the substitute according to Rabbi Ishmael's position are not self- or court-inflicted.[38] The regular, normative obligation for all community members to fast on Yom Kippur along with the illnesses, frustrations, and pains in the normal course of life serve as the symbolic substitute.[39] This feature of atonement is manifested in the fourth and last category mentioned by Rabbi Ishmael—those who profane God's name. Death is their atonement, and it is the death that occurs naturally to every human being.

The symbolic punishment in suffering is a kind of ransom. When it is accompanied by repentance, it establishes an element of sincerity; some price has been paid, though symbolically. The gap between the retributive measure prescribed by the law and the symbolic substitute is bridged by compassion and forgiveness.[40] When that gap is greater, the forgiveness and compassion is deeper. Postulating pain and the internal giving of the self as an alternative to sacrifice overcomes the second anxiety of sacrifice—the crime inherent in the substitution.

Rabbi Ishmael's ingenious approach provides the full spectrum of atonement in two parts. Repentance, the necessary component, is accompanied by a second factor: suffering that symbolizes the actual deserved punishment. In constructing the system of atonement without the substitutive subject of the sacrifice, some self-sacrifice becomes the carrier for substitution. Given other traditions, in which detailed self-inflicted pain and torments or prescribed sufferings serve as the only substitute for a harsher punishment, Rabbi Ishmael's structuring is unique. It draws on the materials of life itself, its pains and end, and transforms them into components of atonement.

Recall that scholars of biblical sacrificial rituals have identified two functions of the blood of sacrifice connected to the double meaning of *kaparah* (atonement): cleansing and ransoming. In establishing suffering as an alternative to sacrifice, the rabbinic literature associates suffering with the same two functions. In addition to the ransoming purpose noted by Rabbi Ishmael in the aforementioned passage, suffering is portrayed as a cleanser, analogous to sacrificial blood.

The humbling effects of pain, the way in which it might sensitize someone to the pain of others, serve as reasons for viewing pain as a form of cathartic purification of the self, or a cathartic experience. In a more direct physical sense, pain is perceived not only as a symptom of illness but also as a necessary component in curing it. Its excruciating burning-like impact is viewed as the means of sanitizing the flesh. The Talmud, for this reason, describes the effects of suffering with the attribute *memarkim* (cleansing):

> R. Simeon b. Lakish said: The word "covenant" is mentioned in connection with salt, and the word "covenant" is mentioned in connection with suffering. . . . Even as in the covenant mentioned in connection with salt, the salt lends a sweet taste to the meat, so also in the covenant mentioned in connection with sufferings, the sufferings wash away ("*memarkim*") all the sins of a human. (Berakhot 5a)

Lemarek means to clean or wipe. It is also used to designate the completion of a process, similar to the way in which polishing is a derivative of wiping. Suffering has a cleansing impact; it wipes the stain of sin. As a metaphor, it doesn't imply an actual ontological stain of sin attached to the sinner and cleansed by pain. Afflictions, in their humbling effect and sensitizing power, are like detergent. In a personal confessional formula that became part of the regular liturgy reported in the Talmud, Raba prayed: "May it be your will God our Lord that I sin no more, and the sins I have committed before You, wipe out ('*marek*') in your great mercies, but not through evil chastisements and diseases" (Berakhot 17a).

Prayer

A distinction must be made between the two senses in which charity and afflictions serve as a replacement for sacrifice. The weaker meaning is that they both achieve the same goal of the sacrifice in a different way. This is the case with the way in which suffering functions as a replacement for the sacrifice. Atonement is reached through pain, but within a different representational structure. While the sacrificial animal stands for the sinner, the symbolic pain stands for the punishment. Suffering also has the cleansing quality of the blood of the sacrifice, but this is a cleansing of the self rather than a purification of the temple. In charity's case, a deeper and stronger sense of replacement emerges. Charity is a gift like the sacrifice, yet since it is given to the outstretched hand of the poor that stands for God's hand, it is an immediate transfer from the giver to the receiver. It thus avoids a feature that will haunt the sacrifice: the immanent gap between giving and receiving. It is a stronger way of replacing sacrifice because it doesn't only fulfill the same goal of the sacrifice; it follows the same structure. With charity, unlike what seems to be the case with pain, there is a transfer, a giver, and a receiver. Charity therefore maintains the essential feature of sacrifice—as an offering.

In a list of personal prayers by Talmudic masters, one prayer is attributed to Rav Sheshet after he kept a fast. An interesting feature of this prayer is that it establishes a pattern in which suffering serves as a strong sense of replacement for structuring sacrifice as a form of transfer:

> When R. Sheshet kept a fast, on concluding his prayer he added the following: Sovereign of the Universe, You know full well that in the time when the Temple was standing, if a man sinned he used to bring a sacrifice, and though all that was offered of it was its fat and blood, atonement was made for him therewith. Now I have kept a fast and my fat and blood have diminished. May it be your will to account my fat and blood which have been diminished as if I had offered them before you on the altar and do though favor me. (Berakhot 17a)

The fat and blood diminished by the fast are looked on as actual entities given from the fasting person to God. This is a higher form of giving, and it points to a shift, expressed in this prayer, from animal sacrifice as a representation *of* the self to an alternative giving through pain, a symbolic sample given *from* the self.

Prayer, the third alternative to sacrifice developed in rabbinic literature, reflects the two senses of replacement discussed above. As a daily structured obligation, prayer emerged in Jewish law only after the temple's destruction, and some of its basic normative structure is organized parallel to the sacrificial system.[41] Prayer served as a replacement in the weaker sense of the term for sacrifice, since through different means, it was perceived to achieve the same goals: atonement, and thank-

ing and appeasing God. The sense in which prayer is a
substitute for animal sacrifice is expressed in the following rabbinic reading of the verse from Hosea: "*Instead of bulls we will pay [The offering of] our lips*"
(Hosea 14:3); "R. Abbahu said: How are we to compensate Thee for the bullocks we used to offer to Thee?
Our lips will pay by means of the prayer we offer to
Thee" (Pesikta de-Rab Kahana, Shuva 24).

The same theme appears in the Midrashic reading of
the verse from the Song of Songs:

> *Thy lips are like a thread of scarlet* this refers to crim-
> son strip. *And thy midbar is comely* this refers to the
> scapegoat. Israel said before the Holy One Blessed be
> He: "Sovereign of the Universe we have neither crim-
> son strip nor scapegoat." He replied: "*Thy lips are like a
> thread of scarlet*: the utterance of thy lips is as beloved
> to me as the strip of crimson." R. Abbahu cited in this
> connection: "*So will we render for the bullocks the of-
> fering of our lips*; what shall we pay in place of bullocks
> and in place of the scapegoat? The utterance of our lips."
> (Shir ha-Shirim Rabba 4:9)

The Midrash reads the scarlet as referring to the red wool
tied to the scapegoat on the Day of Atonement. The wool
string, according to the tradition, turns white to symbol-
ize the people's atonement. The lips, which are read as
indicating the utterances of prayer, are considered a substitute for the atoning force of the ritual. The Midrash
exploits the dual meaning of the word *midbar* in the

verse as well. This word might refer to the desert—that is, the scapegoat sent to the desert—and to the words (*dvarim*) as prayers that substitute for the scapegoat.

These texts seem to point to a stronger, deeper sense of the replacement of sacrifice by prayer. Here, prayer is considered in itself a form of offering, and the words uttered are the objects brought forward before God. Prayer therefore achieves not only the same purpose but also follows the same pattern of the sacrifice.[42] The portrait of prayer itself as an offering emerges more clearly through the image of the words of prayer as "fruits of the lips" laid before God.[43] This image appears in relation to the prayer that is assured in its acceptance:

> Said R. Joshua b. Levi: If a person's lips bore fruit, he is informed that his prayer is accepted. Why is that so [it is said in scripture]: *He creates the fruits of the lips. Peace, peace, to the far and to the near, says the Lord; and I will heal him* [Isaiah 57:18–19]. (Talmud Yerushalmi, Berakhot 5:5)

The fluency of the prayer from the petitioner's lips is a guarantee that the prayer will be accepted. Such fluency is a sign that the prayer itself was inspired and created by God, who according to the verse is the creator of the fruits of the lips. The gap between the giving and receiving is closed when the whole cycle is performed by God himself, who accepts what he gave to begin with; in such a case, there is an identity between the petitioner's and God's will.[44]

The three alternatives to sacrifice—charity, afflictions, and prayer—which were developed in rabbinic literature, maintain the central feature of sacrifice as an offering. And as alternatives, charity and suffering are portrayed as preferable to sacrifice. The preference lies in the fact that in the case of charity, the offering's reception is immediate through the outstretched arm of the poor, and in the case of suffering, the offering is *from* the self, as opposed to the animal sacrifice, which is a substitution *for* the self.

This shift in the locus of the sacrificial drama is reflected in the Midrashic reading of the verse in Psalms: "He who sacrifices thanks giving [*toda*] reveres me and sets out on the proper way" (Ps. 50:23). This translation reads the sacrifice of *todah* as "thanks giving." But the term *toda* lends itself to another interpretation, "confessing," since within biblical language *toda* could mean both thanking and admitting. In this line, the Talmud mentions a reading that sheds new light on the function of confession:

> R. Joshua b. Levi said: he who sacrifices his desire and confesses over it Scripture imputes it to him as though he had honored the Holy One blessed be He in both worlds, this world and the next; for it is written: *He who offers the sacrifice of confession reveres me* (Ps. 50:23).
>
> R. Joshua b. Levi also said: When the Temple was in existence if a man brought a burnt offering he received credit for a burnt offering; if a meal offering, he received

credit for a meal offering; but he who was humble in spirit, Scripture regarded him as though he had brought all the offerings, for it is said, *The sacrifices of God are a broken spirit* [PS. 51:59]. (Babylonian Talmud, Sanhedrin 43b)

Rabbi Joshua's readings present a dramatic shift within sacrifice: the offering is from the self—the sinful desire of the sinner and the pride of the humble in spirit. A person, in offering desire, honors God by granting ultimate priority to his commandments. Such an offering from the self fulfills the task of all sacrifices at once. With this transformation, confession achieves a different meaning. No longer does it designate a substitute for the self, the way it had done with animal sacrifice. In the process of repentance, confession operates as the verbal companion of the offering of desire itself, or in a more direct manner it verbalizes the act of submission, which is the offering of desire.[45] The self becomes the locus of giving. Sacrifice, through pain and prayers as forms of offering, enters a new dimension: self-sacrifice.

Martyrdom, Self-Sacrifice, and Offering

The extension from "sacrificing to" to "sacrificing for" is manifested in the unfolding of the different senses of martyrdom. We can fully grasp this development by exploring the diverse ways in which such self-sacrifice was understood. The most important Talmudic discussion concerning martyrdom raises three distinct themes relating to self-sacrifice and plays out the tension between them. The first context defines the grave conditions under which a person is supposed to sacrifice his life rather than transgress:

> R. Johanan said in the name of R. Simeon b. Jehoza-dak: By a majority vote, it was resolved in the upper chambers of the house of Nithza in Lydda that in every [other] law of the Torah, if a man is commanded: "Transgress and suffer not death" he may transgress and not suffer death, excepting idolatry, incest, and murder. (Babylonian Talmud, Sanhedrin 74a)

The obligation to die is thus reduced solely to three transgressions: murder, incest, and idolatry. A person is not obligated to give up his life in order to fulfill all other obligations and prohibitions.[46]

Following this ruling, the Talmud offers an opposing view, articulating a different context for self-sacrifice:

> Now may not idolatry be practiced [in these circumstances]? Has it not been taught: R. Ishmael said: whence do we know that if a man was bidden, "Engage in idolatry and save your life," that he should do so, and not be slain? From the verse, "*Ye shall therefore keep my statutes and my judgments, which if a man do he shall live in them*": but not die by them. I might think that it may even be openly practiced. But Scripture teaches, "*Neither shall ye profane my holy name; but I will be hallowed*". (Babylonian Talmud, Sanhedrin 74a)

In contrast to the ruling that a person must die rather than engage in idol worship, the Talmud quotes Rabbi Ishmael's position that such an obligation exists only when someone is coerced into public idol worship. A completely new context is therefore applied to self-sacrifice: sanctifying God's name. According to Rabbi Ishmael, in case of idolatry, self-sacrifice is an obligation only under such circumstances, and only when idol worship happens in public. Idolatry in itself, when performed under coercion in private, doesn't constitute a prohibition that has to be adhered to at all costs.[47]

In the martyr's refusal to surrender publicly to the threat of death, the martyr bears witness to the weight and greatness of God's commandment. The impressive resoluteness of the martyr and his calm in the face of death strengthens the spectators' resolve and at times might even convert the executioner. The spectators realize that something of awe-inspiring dimensions is standing before them, irresistible in its conviction. It is thus understandable that the martyr is described in rabbinic literature as someone who sanctifies God's name through this act. This theme concerning self-sacrifice is echoed in the book of the Maccabees from the second century BC—the earliest detailed account of martyrdom, and the earliest one within the Jewish tradition.

By opposing these two very different themes of self-sacrifice, the Talmudic discussion reveals a different orientation toward each of them. In regard to the first theme—the demand to sacrifice life in relation to the severity of the transgression—the Talmud has a tendency to significantly mitigate the demand for self-sacrifice.[48] It states that only three transgressions carry such weight. Preserving life is an overriding value. A person doesn't have to give up his life for the sake of a commandment such as preserving the Sabbath. In respect to the second theme—self-sacrifice for sanctifying God's name—the Talmud moves in a different direction. While Rabbi Ishmael mentions the value of self-sacrifice only in relation to the public coercion of idol worship, seeing idolatry as the only proper spectacular stage for such an act, the Talmud quotes the following third-century statements, dramatically expanding the category:

> When R. Dimi came he said: This was taught only if there is no royal decree, but if there is a royal decree, one must incur martyrdom rather than transgress even a minor precept. When Rabin came, he said in R. Johanan's name: Even without a royal decree, it was only permitted in private; but in public one must be martyred even for a minor precept rather than violate it. What is meant by a "minor precept"?—Raba son of R. Isaac said in Rab's name: Even to change one's shoe strap. (Babylonian Talmud, Sanhedrin 74a–b)

When coercion occurs during a large-scale attempt at forced conversion, or in public, self-sacrifice is demanded concerning all matters. The obligation to sanctify God's name and resist such pressure has a leveling quality. Even the most minor of issues turns out to be a case for principled resolute opposition. While the obligation for self-sacrifice was reduced to only three exceptional matters when concerned with the severity of the transgression itself, it was extended to include even the smallest of all matters in the case of bearing public witness and withstanding religious coercion.

The third theme of self-sacrifice relates to love. In its effort to ground the obligation to sacrifice one's life rather than worship idols in private (contrary to Rabbi Ishmael's opinion above), the Talmud notes:

> For it has been taught, R. Eliezer said: "*And thou shalt love the Lord thy God with all thy heart and with all thy soul, and with all thy might.*" Since with all thy soul is stated, why is with all thy might stated? Or if with all thy might be written, why also write with all thy soul? For the man to whom life is more precious than wealth, with all thy soul is written; whilst he to whom wealth is more precious than life is bidden, with all thy might [i.e., substance]. (Babylonian Talmud, Sanhedrin 74a)

The martyr also expresses his ultimate love of God through an exhibition of unconditional and noninstrumental loyalty to him.[49] Such martyrdom doesn't necessarily need an audience; it therefore, as the Talmud understood it, is practiced in private as well.

The theme of such love as the ultimate expression of worship and height of the religious stance is at the center of the accounts about Rabbi Akiba's martyrdom at the hands of the Romans:

> When R. Akiba was taken out for execution, it was
> the hour for the recital of the *Shema'*, and while they
> combed his flesh with iron combs, he was accepting
> upon himself the kingship of heaven. His disciples said
> to him: Our teacher, even to this point? He said to them:
> All my days I have been troubled by this verse, *with all
> thy soul,* [which I interpret,] "even if He takes thy soul."
> I said: When shall I have the opportunity of fulfilling
> this? Now that I have the opportunity shall I not ful-
> fill it? He prolonged the word "ehad" until he expired
> while saying it. (Babylonian Talmud, Berakhot 61b)

This expression of love well exceeds the emphasis on
the severity of the particular prohibition that must
be preserved at all costs. Rabbi Akiba is portrayed as
someone who craved such a moment all his life. It is
also a moment that surpasses the concern with the effect of sanctifying God's name on the audience, though
it might have had a great impact. Akiba's martyrdom
had the private quality of love, an event that even if coerced by executioners in the presence of witnesses, was
essentially an intimate moment.

Although I have insisted on using the term "self-
sacrifice" to refer to these three distinct themes, none of
them has actually been described in the variety of Talmudic and Midrashic texts as sacrifice (*korban*). They
instead are phrased as "get killed rather than transgress"
(*yehareg ve'al ya'avor*), "sanctify God's name" (*le-kadesh
et hashem*), or "love of God with all the soul." "Self-

sacrifice" is not a recognizable category in these earlier texts, since as I mentioned, the conjunction "sacrifice for" emerged in Hebrew, as in other languages, much later than "sacrifice to." At that stage, the term *korban* referred solely to a gift as an offering that is given from one domain to another domain.

Another stage in the history of martyrdom had to occur before the extension from "sacrifice to" to "sacrifice for" could have happened. The understanding of martyrdom itself as an actual offering of the self to God served as a crucial link. Such understanding meant that the martyr was considered not only as dying for the sake of not transgressing the gravest of all prohibitions, the public witnessing of one's steadfast faith in God, or as an expression of absolute loyalty and love, but rather as an offering, a gift offered by the martyr—the gift of himself—to God.

In the second book of Maccabees, the earliest detailed account of martyrdom, and the subsequent rabbinic literature, death for the sake of God was rarely and marginally portrayed in terms of offering the self to God in the form of sacrifice.[50] The equation of this form of self-sacrifice with an actual offering to God emerged as a key theme among the early Christian martyrs. At the beginning of the second century, Ignatius of Antioch, in his *Epistle to the Romans*, described the martyr's flesh devoured by the wild beasts as the "pure bread of Christ."[51] And Origen made an explicit analogy between the martyrs' self-sacrifice and the sacrificial animals offered to God that are mentioned in Leviticus. This unique transformation of the meaning of self-sacrifice in martyrdom into an actual offering is a way of depicting the Christian martyrs not only as witnessing the truth of their belief in Christ but also as emulating him as an offering to God, while their self-sacrifice has the same purifying and atoning impact as his.

As Guy Stroumsa points out, the end of animal sacrifice fostered the understanding of martyrdom as an offering, and martyrdom emerged as a substitute for it.[52] Unlike the other three substitutes discussed so far—charity, suffering, and prayer—martyrdom as a substitute for the temple sacrifice had a more direct, paradoxical aspect. Since animal sacrifice was considered, to begin with, a substitute for the giving of the self, martyrdom was a substitute that aimed at short-circuiting that kind of substitution by directly offering the self. In that respect, such substitution has the potential of once and for all putting an end to animal sacrifice as Christianity understood it, rather than temporarily replacing temple worship until conditions allowed it to resume.

In Jewish sources, possibly as a result of Christian influence, the view of the martyr as a sacrificial offering emerged as a main theme only after the temple's destruction but at a later stage—from around the seventh century onward.[53] In its fullest and most important formulation, the offering theme appeared in the *Story of the Ten Martyrs*, which became a crucial source for the Jewish martyrological tradition of Ashkenaz and was incorporated into the Yom Kippur liturgy. Rabbi Ishmael, the central figure among the ten martyrs, ascends to heaven before all their deaths at the hands of the Romans, and the angel Gabriel describes to him the heavenly altar that exists parallel to the earthly one in the temple. Ishmael then inquires about the nature of the sacrifices that are offered there: "He asked him: 'And what do you sacrifice on it? Do you have cows, rams and sheep?' He answered him: 'We sacrifice the souls of the righteous upon it.'"[54] The ten great scholars, like other souls of the martyred righteous, are destined to serve as offerings to God's altar.

In the Jewish chronicles of martyrdom during the first and second Crusades, sacrificial language becomes common to describe the Jewish martyrs. The death of Jews by the Crusaders is depicted as a sacrificial offering, and the killing of children by their parents in order to avoid forced conversion is portrayed as an enactment of the binding of Isaac, the *akedah*, with the full language of the sacrificial temple rites.[55] In his eulogy for the Ashkenazi communities destroyed in the second Crusade, Ephraim of Bonn spoke of the quality of the Ashkenazi martyrs in the following words: "The glory of the martyrs is greater than that of the high priest. He sprinkled the blood of the (animal) sacrifices and they sprinkled their own blood and the blood of their dear children. And they have bound the bindings, and built altars and prepared slaughtering."[56]

It seems that once the martyr's death was construed as an offering, a new horizon in the understanding of sacrifice emerged: "sacrificing for." Moreover, the category of self-sacrifice as an offering was extended to acts that did not necessarily involve a transfer of something to someone. Sacrifice began to designate not only *giving to* but also *giving up* (for the sake of). The concept of sacrifice can thus be expanded from the religious realm, which involved a god, the receiving subject at the other end of the offering, to the ethical and political realm. At this stage in the history of sacrifice, it is proper to move the discussion from "sacrificing to" to "sacrificing for."

Sacrificing for

ℰℛℴ

Self-Transcendence and Violence

Self-transcendence is at the core of the human capacity for a moral life. The movement of the self to self-transcendence has been articulated in different ways in the history of philosophy: adopting the perspective of the other, such as in the golden rule, "what is hateful to you do not do to your neighbor"; the identification of the individual with the general will in Rousseau's social contract; universalizing the maxim of action as a test for its morality in Kant's categorical imperative; viewing oneself as one among many in granting equal weight to every unit of utility in utilitarianism; locating the self behind the veil of ignorance in John Rawls's original position, which secures inferring the principles of justice without the biases of individual interests; Thomas Nagel's distinction between agent-relative actions and rules that give a place to the particular concerns of an agent's interest, and agent-neutral rules that do not give any weight to an agent's interests. All of these attempts seem to share a basic intuition considered essential to moral life: the assumption that without the self freeing himself from his particular interested point of view, there is no moral life.

These positions share a certain moral psychology that defines the nature of moral conflict and drama as well. People have a strong initial tendency toward self-privileging, which stands in conflict with self-transcendence. This inclination to privilege one's own concerns might be rooted in deep biological organic factors in which people are motivated by the primary instincts of self-preservation and -gratification. Self-regarding tendencies also might be grounded in failures of the imagination, the narrow horizons of attention that sometimes are constituted by habit, and defensive and self-deceptive mechanisms that blind people to the pleas of others. The conception of the moral life as founded by self-transcendence, coupled with the background condition of a strong self-privileging tendency, undergirds Kant's description of the conflict as the struggle between self-love and the categorical imperative. Freudian moral psychologists define this conflict as the struggle between the id and the super ego. Whatever the particular terms, all those who share this broad moral outlook of self-transcendence as the basis of morality along with the conflict between self-transcendence and self-interest as the heart of the moral drama perceive sacrifice as an essential component of the moral life.[1]

Sacrifice's place in moral life also serves as a scale for measuring the weight of moral demands and obligations in two ways. The first scale measures the relative weight of moral obligations through examining judgments about cases in which two moral obligations clash with one another. In such conflicts, the weightier demand will be defined as the one that overrides the other. Reasonable people will claim, for example, that a person ought to lie in order to save someone's life. The obligation to save life is said to be weightier than the prohibition against telling a lie. The second scale measures the degree of the sacrifice required for fulfilling an obligation. Unlike the first measure, which weighs intramoral conflicts, the second assesses the clash between moral demands and the agent's interests. The weightier the demand, the greater the sacrifice expected. If the demand is absolute—that is, if it ought to be adhered to at any cost—it might make a claim for the ultimate sacrifice: the obligation to forfeit one's life. An example might be the prohibition against murder. One can well imagine a case in which someone decides to sacrifice his own life rather than intentionally kill an innocent person who does not pose a threat to his life.

This second measure allows us to rank the order of moral obligations in terms of the expected degree of personal sacrifice—for instance, the prospect of self-sacrifice in order to save someone's life compared to self-sacrifice in order to avoid killing an innocent person. The mainstream view in Jewish law is that a person may be obligated to risk or give up his life so as not to kill an innocent person, but may not be expected to give up his life to save another. Examining the expected sacrifice in such a case is a way to explore the relative different moral weights of action and omission.

Many of the debates and arguments among contemporary moral philosophers are driven by sensitivity to this structure of moral conflict and the possible consuming power of moral demand. Philosophers have criticized utilitarianism for granting more weight to overall utility maximization than to agent-relative considerations in the moral calculus. The demand that every action should be guided by the attempt to maximize the overall utility is experienced as a moral environmental hazard. If it were followed meticulously, it might leave its follower with the bare skeleton of an ordinary subsistence life while the rest would be devoted to piety.[2] In confronting the sacrifice and demand that is postulated by morality, philosophers have also debated whether morality ought to be the overriding factor in every circumstance.[3] Those who assume that it is have also argued about the scope of moral demand—a fraught question in light of the overwhelming amount of pain and suffering in the world.[4] Yet despite the variety of philosophical approaches to the problem, all share the view that the clash between self-transcendent, agent-neutral claims and the concerns of self-interest is at the heart of moral conflict, and that moral life demands sacrifice.

But not all philosophers subscribe to this consensus. Postulating that self-transcendence is at the core of moral life commits one to a Kantian stance toward moral life. Moral philosophers who adopt competing approaches—

the Hobbesian one, with its tracing of moral life back to a combination of self-interest and instrumental rationality; the Aristotelian version, which grounds the ethical life in a conception of self-flourishing; or the Nietzschean approach, which views self-transcendence and sacrifice as a perverse and destructive application of the will to power on the self—will take issue with this Kantian perspective. The list of challengers is indeed impressive. I think that they are all misguided, but I cannot argue this position here. I will instead accept this picture as a given, and attempt to unravel what I take to be a central tension within this outlook with far-reaching implications in three areas. The first relates to the way in which we understand the role of sacrifice in moral conflict; the second is in regard to self-sacrifice and the morality of war and just-war theories; and the third pertains to the relationship between self-transcendence and the political order.

I

Among those who see self-transcendence as being at the root of morality, it is assumed that our capacity to restrain our self-interest puts a check on our tendencies toward violence. The phenomenon of war, as perhaps the most extreme manifestation of violence that humanity has ever invented, forces us to think through and refine this presupposition. War is a complex mixture of self-sacrifice and brutality, and thus it brings out that which is most noble and debased in our nature. The talent for self-sacrifice that is essential to war is in much greater supply than is commonly presumed. In the course of the twentieth century, sacrificial resources—otherwise known, cynically, as cannon fodder—were recruited in unlimited quantities. Millions of young men—Japanese, Germans, French, Russians, British, and Americans, among others—readily made themselves available for self-sacrifice.

The ease with which war planners have been able to mobilize masses of soldiers ready to make the ultimate sacrifice is cause for reflection. The warmongers' success is not because of appeals to the id, or some other instinct rooted in or directed by the pleasure principle. The pleasure principle and self-interest more generally are overrated in ordinary moral psychology. Self-interest can certainly drive us to crimes that are animal-like. But war involves more spectacular crimes, greater in scope and horror, and not merely because the technological means of waging war have become increasingly lethal. The horror of war can also be traced back to the quality of the warrior's motivations. Human beings are the only species that kills for principle rather then for self-interest. What I want to claim in establishing the connection between sacrifice and violence is that war is not embarked on despite the risk and sacrifice that it involves; it is strengthened and motivated by this aspect. There is, in other words, a deep internal (and not accidental) connection between killing and self-sacrifice. Two reversals are key to this internal connection.

First and foremost, the connection between self-sacrifice and violence is established through a dangerous yet common reversal between two claims: since it is the mark of the good that it deserves sacrifice, the reverse must be true too—namely, that sacrifice makes something into a good. This is how the spectacle of brave soldiers casting aside their own self-interest and putting themselves at risk leads to a form of moral self-deception that is difficult to avoid.

Ivan Kaliayev, the hero of Albert Camus play *The Just Assassin*, embodies this logic to its bitter end. Kaliayev, a revolutionary socialist who has assassinated Grand Duke Sergey, uncle of the Russian czar, refuses to accept a pardon for his act. In his opinion, his violence will be vindicated only when he himself is executed. To the offer of pardon proposed to him in prison by the grand duchess, he answers, "If I don't die, then I'll be a murderer." And in his speech at his trial, he proclaims, "If I've reached the summit of human resistance to violence, then may death crown my works by proving the purity of my belief." Kaliayev's willingness to die is not motivated by the quest for atonement. Rather, he understands his future execution as a retroactive justification for the assassination. Kaliayev wants to die because he is convinced that his death would redeem the act from the charge of selfishness; it would purify it and immunize him from all blame.

There is yet another revealing element in Camus's play that concerns the connection between self-sacrifice and violence. In embracing his own execution, Kaliayev bears witness as well to the claim that the cause is worthy of sacrificing one's life, and hence the grand duke's death was justified. Had Kaliayev not supported his own execution, we might suspect that his conviction that the cause is worthier than life itself is only true concerning someone else's life. In giving up his life, the conviction seems more genuine. This deep connection between self-sacrifice and sanctification is expressed in one of the play's dramatic dialogues. Dora, a co-conspirator and an ex-lover of Kaliayev, encourages him to be tried and executed: "We are obliged to kill, right? We deliberately sacrifice one life and only one? . . . But first to go to the assassination and then to the gallows, is to give your life twice. We pay more than we owe." Kaliayev, in turn, reaffirms this viewpoint: "Yes that is to die twice. . . . No one can criticize us. Now I am sure of myself." The problem with this logic is the too-facile leap from the worthiness of giving up a life for a cause to according oneself license to take a life for that cause.

This phenomenon is rooted in another deeper, more convoluted form of reversal that occurs when the practice of self-sacrifice generates a reversal of perpetrator and victim. A grotesque example of this shift was manifested in Heinrich Himmler's speech to his SS officers. In describing the authorization for the Final Solution, Himmler made the following declaration: "The order to solve the Jewish question, this was the most frightening order an organization could ever receive." One wonders, of course, frightening for whom? Himmler clearly meant the organization, not the Jews. In another part of his speech, he asserted: "We realize that what we are expecting from you is superhuman, to be superhumanly inhuman."[5] Himmler portrayed his officers as selfless beings who made the ultimate sacrifice. Their victims may have lost their lives, but the SS officers paid the highest price in sacrificing their conscience for a greater goal: the overcoming of their humanity. Morality, in this view, is a great temptation to be overcome in the name of a higher mission. Those who conquered the temptation and withstood the trial turned out to be the real victims of their own crimes.

What is astonishing about such a substitution of roles is that no actual self-sacrifice has to occur. The acknowledgment of the inhumanity of the act itself internally carries its sacrificial dimension. To this twisted reversal a final perversion was added with Himmler's self-congratulatory remark: "To have stuck it out and, apart from exceptions caused by human weakness, to have remained decent, that is what has made us hard. This is a page of glory in our history which has never been written and is never to be written."[6]

This reversal highlights one of the complicated functions of guilt as self-punishment. Guilt, as an emotional response, is necessary for any moral behavior and personality. It nevertheless can play a narcissistic role by giving license to the perpetrator to turn himself into the victim. The aggressor, wallowing in his guilt, sees himself as suffering from a far greater harm than that inflicted by his own blows. He identifies those whom he has hurt as responsible for this pain. For this reason, he deeply resents those whom he has harmed. He sees them as his tormentors.

Such was the case in the Bible with Amnon, the son of King David, who was infatuated with his sister Tamar and raped her. The verse in the book of Samuel describes how Amnon's love turned into hate after the rape and humiliation: "Then Amnon hated her with exceeding great hatred; for the hatred wherewith he hated her was greater than the love wherewith he had loved her" (II Sam. 13:15). Tamar became a living reminder of Amnon's own crime. Rather than evoking regret and compassion, her continued presence was torturous for Amnon, who made her his enemy.

The mind can play complicated games, and among them is the accusation that an aggressor directs toward his victim for causing him to become violent, which all too easily turns into a justification for further violence. This cycle seems to be an integral feature of abuse. A person who feels guilty toward someone begins to see that person as his tormentor, which gives him a reason for further aggression, causing an escalation of guilt, which in turn provides the rationale for more aggression. This cycle is common in ongoing conditions of closeness and symbiosis where the aggressor identifies his victim with his baser instincts.

Guilt, as an instrument of reversal, has an even finer quality. It bears immediate witness to the perpetrator's righteousness. Since guilt is self-inflicted, it is not a punishment delivered from an outside force; it is a sign of the aggressor's sensitivity and virtue. The circle of reversal is therefore completed. The guilty party is not only the actual victim but also a righteous victim.

In religious traditions, and in the ways in which Kierkegaard and other thinkers interpret them, a troubling expansion of the concept of sacrifice is relevant to this structure. The giving of or from the self is hailed, as was pointed out in the previous section, as an expression of loyalty and love. Asceticism as a value is sometimes based on this concept of giving of the self. Yet one can also note how the notion of sacrifice moves beyond the giving up of desires, instincts, and goals, toward the sacrifice of moral conscience. The story in Genesis of Abraham's trial, in which God commands him to sacrifice his beloved son Isaac, became a paradigm case of the expansion of sacrifice to morality itself. In the name of faith, Abraham, as Kierkegaard puts it, suspended the ethical.[7] He was willing to sacrifice his moral obligation as a father in order to follow God's will. It is important, though, to stress that in this "sacrifice" of moral conscience, the one who was actually sacrificed (or who would have been sacrificed had God not intervened at the last minute) was another human being. Though Abraham had to overcome his moral conviction, the real victim of the story is Isaac, not Abraham. Isaac would have been slaughtered in the end. More generally, when morality is depicted as a temptation to be surmounted in the name of a higher goal, it is always someone else who pays the price. It is a rather perverse moment in some religious traditions to view the victim as the one who sacrificed his moral principles. In such cases, the very fact of sacrifice purifies a crime with the illusion that the criminal is the victim since he has sacrificed his conscience.

Self-sacrifice, with all its subtleties and complexities, enables violence because it allows a role reversal between the aggressor and victim. The contemporary suicide bomber is a complex icon of such a merger of violence and self-sacrifice. In his act of unleashing violence, the suicide bomber is simultaneously initiating an act of self-sacrifice and murder. He constitutes himself as the victim of the violence that he is perpetrating. The suicide bomber is presumably an effective tactical instrument—a human version of a high-tech smart bomb. Yet despite the surface efficiency of the act, suicide bombing is a powerful cultural statement, a simultaneous image of self-sacrifice and murder, a perverse conjunction of blood and purity, crime and atonement. It is no accident that the suicide bomber emerges from a larger politics of victimhood. This internal connection between self-sacrifice and violence along with the reversals that self-sacrifice enables do not belong exclusively to the religious sphere. War, which manifests such a connection, has been practiced in thoroughly secularized nation-states, and Camus's just assassin is a secular socialist.[8]

A deep inner tension is thus evident in the noble ideal of self-transcendence. Through two reversals, self-sacrifice mobilizes crimes that in their magnitude are far greater than those motivated by self-interest. This phenomenon forces a critical reformulation of the nature of moral conflict, especially in light of Kant's view that the essence of moral conflict is the struggle between self-love and the categorical imperative.[9] By posing this polarity, Kant ignored the realm at the core of moral drama: self-sacrifice—by no means an expression of self-love, and yet also unable to fulfill the demands of the universalized categorical imperative. In order to fully explain the deficiency of Kant's moral psychology and the alternative to his account, some clarification of his concept of self-love is important.

Kant's concept of self-love is far richer and more complex than the mere sphere of actions that are performed for the sake of meeting urges and passions. The conflict between self-love and the categorical imperative is thus not the superficial clash between altruism and carnal satisfaction. According to Kant, a person who is moved to act by the sheer force of his drives is not an agent, and an action in the full sense of the word is not yet ascribed to him. Only when he adopts the fulfillment of his interests as his principle of action does he establish a genuine tension between self-love and the categorical imperative. For such conflict to occur in its fullness, an agent ought to adopt the following principle: "The fulfillment of actions that are rooted in self-love are of utmost importance to me and I will therefore opt to act in such a way that will enhance my self-interests." If this is the overriding and absolute principle for the agent, we confront a manifestation of evil.[10]

Even more so, in his concept of self-love Kant includes actions that a human being performs not only for fulfilling bodily passions. The category also includes interests that have their source in "spiritual" ambitions such as the desire for superiority over other human beings and the threat that someone might feel when he perceives himself as inferior. Moral conflict, then, might be motivated by not only carnal passions but spite, resentment, and envy as well.[11] The self might be defined in an expansive way too, so that the category of self-love then includes the interests of the group with which an individual identifies himself. The altruistic action of a parent for the sake of his children might, according to Kant, be motivated by self-love.

Kant extended the category even further to include actions that are performed out of compassion for others with whom the self doesn't identify. And yet for Kant, self-love is not a mere residual category that refers to every principle and action that does not fit the categorical imperative. What will define an action as an expression of self-love—even when done for the sake of another human being, including a complete stranger—is the fact that it is motivated not by the categorical imperative but instead by the pleasure that a person will derive from helping someone else. In other words, the agent who recognizes himself as a compassionate creature predicts that an action for the other's sake will give him pleasure, and the purpose of such action is self-love. His action is motivated by a calculation of the future happiness he will experience as a result of the happiness of the person he is helping.[12]

Thus, Kant had a rather complex and sophisticated concept of self-love, and yet a great and significant space still remains between self-love and the obedience to the categorical imperative. Within that space, which Kant didn't recognize, stands the most meaningful arena of moral conflict. A person who sacrifices his interest for the sake of God, the working class, or the homeland doesn't necessarily act from a sense of expansion of his own self, which includes the whole of the God, the working class, or the nation. It likewise would be wrong to argue that this person is motivated by the pleasure that he expects from furthering the aims of his sacrifice. The opposite seems to be more accurate: owing to the value he attributes to the ideal for which he sacrifices, he might anticipate that such sacrifice will bring him happiness. He doesn't choose to sacrifice because he predicts it will bring him happiness; he opts to sacrifice solely for the value he attributes to the cause, and whatever happiness he expects will merely be a by-product of helping to bring it about. Such self-transcendent actions, which might provide the basis for horrible crimes, are therefore not expressions of self-love. Similarly, they do not fulfill the criteria set by the categorical imperative, since it is impossible to generalize a violent act done for the sake of God, the working class, or the nation as a universal maxim of action.

A broad arena of actions—unmotivated by self-love yet fundamentally shaped by self-transcendence—exists in the space between self-love and the universal categorical imperative; on the other hand, these actions are not an expression of the categorical imperative's fulfillment. Within that space of self-transcendence, between self-love and the categorical imperative, one finds the most meaningful and deepest aspect of moral conflict.

The moral drama and its psychology have to be reformulated: *misguided self-transcendence is morally more problematic and lethal than a disproportionate attachment to self-interest.* In line with a long philosophical tradition, I think that self-transcendence does constitute the moral act. But from that fact itself, self-sacrifice also derives its corrupting force. Misdirected self-transcendence falsely stimulates a noble moral act, and with that it enables a complex mechanism, based on the two reversals, to purify crimes. The religious sensitivity to such a phenomenon is the reason why misguided self-transcendence constitutes the ultimate sin of idolatry. Idolatry, in this sense, is the utmost surrender to a cause that is not worthy of the corresponding sacrifice.

War and the Sacrificial Logic

In his penetrating phenomenology of the sacrificial aspect of political violence, Paul Kahn observes that "the double aspect of sacrifice—self and other—continues to this day. One can take another life only when one is willing to give up one's own."[13] This connection, magnified by the suicide bomber, is not a mere psychological self-deceptive mechanism; it actually might penetrate the deepest strata of both the morality and laws of war. In order to consider the potential relationship between self-sacrifice and violence in war, it is necessary to briefly explore the laws of war.

Just war theory and the law of war are based on two basic distinctions. The first and most important is the exclusion of civilians from a war zone in two ways: civilians don't constitute legitimate targets, and soldiers can only aim intentionally directed fire at other combatants; and civilians cannot take part in the hostilities, and they are not allowed to participate in a war unless they identify themselves as soldiers by wearing distinct uniforms and openly carrying arms. Anyone who fights against soldiers of an enemy army without wearing a military uniform is not considered a soldier. If captured, he is treated as a criminal rather than a prisoner of war. Soldiers, on the other hand, form part of a war zone in two senses: they represent legitimate targets and intentional fire can be aimed at them; and they have the legitimate right to participate in the fighting and kill enemy soldiers as long as they abide by the rules of war.

The norm of excluding civilians from war and including soldiers is reinforced by another modern distinction in the laws of war—the principle of independence, which states that the rigid separation between civilians and soldiers applies regardless of the circumstances under which the war started. In maintaining a firm divide between *jus ad bellum* (the justice of the war) and *jus in bello* (just conduct in the war), the common view is that soldiers have a right to kill one another regardless of whether they are engaged in a just war or not, as long as they fight in a just way and abide by the rules of *jus in bello*. This right, referred to as "belligerent privilege," implies that soldiers may be targeted even if they are fighting against an unjust aggressor. The divide applies to civilians as well. Civilians may not be targeted even if they belong to the aggressor's state that initiated an unjust war, and they cannot participate in fighting even if they are fighting against an unjust aggressor.

This structure seems to be supported by a powerful intuition: civilians ought to stay outside the war equation, and it is prohibited to harm them intentionally, since they do not pose any threat. Killing civilians, even if it promotes the aims of a just war, is murderous because they are innocent, even though they are members of the enemy's camp. Soldiers, on the other hand, become legitimate targets by making themselves dangerous; they pose a threat.[14] This logic makes perfect sense when dealing with the question of who can become a legitimate target. But it gets more complicated when grappling with who has a right to participate in the war and who has the legitimate right to kill. In examining this side of the equation, we find that the willingness to self-sacrifice might play what seems to me a perverse role.

Let me start with the assertion that a civilian is outside the war equation not only as a target but also as a participant. According to this rule, a civilian may not participate in a war even against an unjust aggressor. What follows from this point of view, for example, is the notion that it was appropriate to deny a member of the French underground, disguising himself in civilian garb while fighting against the Nazis, all the protections granted to a soldier at the time. There might be an argument for such a rule, since civilians are not trusted to make judgments concerning the question of whether the war is just or not, and therefore there is a need to legislate a total prohibition against civilian participation in hostilities, especially when such participation endangers other innocent civilians. Such a claim insists that if we wish to exclude civilians from the battlefield, it is imperative that soldiers feel safe among civilians, and a concealed attack undermines such an essential concern.[15] Disguised combatants cannot receive the protections afforded to soldiers.

But another argument connected to self-sacrifice might play a role in such a prohibition. The soldier who dons a military uniform and thus puts his life on the line is understood to have earned the right, so to speak, of inflicting harm or even death. Combatants who are disguised as civilians, conversely, do not present themselves as potential targets, and since they don't risk themselves, they are not allowed to risk others' lives. This insight was behind criticisms of the US government's decision in the 1990s to order high-altitude bombing missions during the Kosovo crisis. Critics alleged that since there was no risk to the pilots, the bombers didn't have the right to place other lives in jeopardy.[16] I find this contention puzzling. Demanding risk as a condition for soldiering might be good policy to reduce fighting (by increasing the cost of becoming a soldier). Sometimes the desire to avoid risk costs civilian lives—Serbian ones, in the case of Kosovo, since high-altitude bombings are far less accurate. Under such circumstances, it is a legitimate moral demand to expect soldiers to assume risk in order to avoid even unintentionally killing civilians. Risk for its own sake as a justification for the "right" to take life seems questionable, though. If the war is just, why should the soldier put himself at risk in trying to protect either himself or others?

The same connection between self-sacrifice and killing might play a troubling role in the inclusion of soldiers in a war zone. According to widely held theories of justice in war, soldiers who confront one another on both sides of the front have a symmetrical moral right to kill one another. This is true regardless of the justness of the war itself. Such soldiers, as Michael Walzer describes it, "face one another as moral equals."[17] Each can kill the other in self-defense, as long as each identifies himself as a threat to the other. The claim for moral symmetry between combatants assumes the following logic. While confronting one another on the battlefield, both armies pose a threat to one another; both have the right to defend themselves against the other as long as they aim their fire at the ones who pose a threat to them. It is essential to maintaining the integrity of such a structure that each side put itself at potential risk, because without it neither can claim to be defending himself. Both parties, by simultaneously threatening to and being threatened by each other, establish a moral equilibrium among themselves. The symmetry of this assertion of self-defense thus presupposes a basic element of risk and self-sacrifice at its core.

There are difficulties with this argument, however, particularly in the case of an unjust war, and the grounds for such moral equality, if there is such equality, have to be carefully deciphered. Soldiers fighting on the side that began a war with no just cause are presumably criminal, even if they limit their violence only to the soldiers on the opposite side. Their self-imposed limitation is not sufficient to legitimate the fighting. The fact that enemy soldiers threaten them on the front itself doesn't grant the aggressors the right of self-defense. Instead, the aggressors have the obligation to retreat. If we factor in the background conditions that brought the soldiers into this mutually threatening situation, there cannot be a reciprocal right to self-defense. The duty to disarm—or cease and desist—applies to any aggressor who attacks with unjust cause. Hence, although one can well imagine how a just war could be fought unjustly, there is no way to fight an unjust war in a just manner.

One might object to this characterization by pointing out that the ordinary foot soldier plays no role, personally, in instigating the unjust war. On the contrary, he is compelled to fight, and in some cases even threatened with imprisonment or physical violence if he doesn't fight. Yet this fact alone does not place him on the same moral plane as the soldiers fighting for the attacked country. Let me illustrate this idea. A threatens B that he will kill him if he doesn't kill C. B is morally prohibited from taking C's life. Let us assume that B, faced with this awful predicament and wanting to do the right thing, decides to arrange a duel with C. He grants C the right to defend himself and thereby creates a situation in which C is given an opportunity to threaten B's life. Although B may be tempted to claim the right to self-defense, the claim would be illegitimate. B's obligation, in this case, is to retreat or submit. It is certainly morally preferable that B give C the chance to save himself. Nevertheless, the source of the moral preference is not the fact that B is willing to risk his life but rather that C has a chance to save himself. (The duel case will be morally equivalent to a case in which B decided to use an old, unreliable gun with a lower probability of hitting the target, thus giving C a greater chance to escape harm.) In sum, the aggressor does not gain the right of self-defense by giving the victimized party the power to harm him.[18] If the aggressor assumes that by giving the other the chance to kill him, he gained the right to kill the other, he is trapped in the illusion that willingness to sacrifice might create a right.

Another argument might be raised to justify the moral equality of combatants. Combatants are usually not in a position to obtain the proper information to help them form a serious evaluation of the justice of the war. Their state feeds them its own narrow viewpoint, which distorts their judgment. It would be unfair to expect them to weigh the rationales while being drafted when it is clear that they don't have the appropriate information for such an evaluation. Although such a contention might provide an *excuse* for many combatants in many wars, it doesn't offer a *justification* for the moral equality of soldiers.[19] If we don't consider the mutual risk as a genuine source of equivalence between soldiers, since self-sacrifice shouldn't grant an action a justification, we are faced with the following argument: Soldiers fighting according to the rules of war are not criminals and they have the protection granted to soldiers, yet there is no moral equality between soldiers on both sides in an unjust war, since one side has a justification to fight and the other has a mere excuse. We might, for good reasons, decide that this gap should not create a legal difference and each side will be granted belligerent privileges, but there is, morally speaking, a huge difference between them.

The counterargument is that not all wars look like the Wehrmacht's march into Poland, where it was clear who the unjust party was. There are wars in which both sides seem to have reasonable claims against the other, wars in which it is unclear who initiated the aggression, and conflicts in which the cause has long been forgotten, although the killing continues through sheer inertia. In such harder cases, one might suggest, an actual symmetrical right of self-defense exists. Analogously, two strangers arriving at a theater's box office at the same time could each claim to be the first in line for tickets. Should their disagreement degenerate into threats and blows, each would appear to have the right of self-defense. Despite these seemingly plausible scenarios, I don't think there is ever a symmetrical right to self-defense; the party's true obligation is compromise. If one side wishes to compromise and the other doesn't, the intransigent side loses its right to self-defense and should be held responsible for initiating any act of violence. If both sides refuse to compromise, they are both guilty.

A justification rather than an excuse for a version of the moral equality of combatants might be found in a contention that doesn't assume the role of threats and putting oneself at risk as sufficient sources of symmetry. Analogies from individual cases of self-defense to the collective nature of war are of limited use.[20] In war, a soldier is committed not only to his own self-defense but also to the defense of his comrades, family, and state. He will act in their defense even if he is completely secure and safe, and even if the enemy he is attacking might pose no threat to him. Warfare is not an aggregate of individual confrontations; soldiers are committed to their fellow citizens' well-being and their state's security as a common pursuit. I therefore need to refine the analogy. Let me add a character, D, to the previous example. D and B are close friends. Should D join B when B defends himself against C, even though B initiated an unjust fight? This is a complex situation of a conflict between associational obligations and the rights of strangers to life. There might be a serious claim here that in such a situation, after D's failure to convince B to stop the fight, he is justified in joining B to defend himself against C.[21] The moral equality of D and C, as they confront one another, is not based on D's willingness to sacrifice himself but rather on the fact that his friend B is under an actual threat and he feels compelled to defend him.

In cases of collective efforts such as war, this associational obligation goes deeper. It is aimed at not only protecting fellow soldiers but also granting long-term stability and viability to shared political life as such. The terms of solidarity between citizens in a democracy are expressed in the normative expectation that citizens voluntarily abide by the decisions of a democratically elected government, even if they deeply disagree. In decisions pertaining to war, such a commitment means risking one's life for a war deemed to be unnecessary and wrong. Such citizens will act against their most heartfelt convictions, with the expectation that in the event they manage to convince the public and become a majority, the minority will reciprocate with the same posture of solidarity. Without such shared willingness, the civic bond will unravel altogether and the state's capacity to function will be seriously challenged.

Yet this notion can be questioned. Soldiers' associational obligations toward one another and their fellow citizens don't override the human rights of the civilians on the other side. Intentionally killing civilians in order to save your own citizens and soldiers by putting pressure on the enemy to end a war is rightfully considered a war crime. What, then, is the difference between the civilian and the soldier? Why should an associational obligation override the defending soldier's right to life, since it is agreed that it doesn't override the rights of civilians? It might be claimed that the soldier has forfeited his right to life because he is a danger to others, but in an unjust attack, this role was forced on him. It is true that attacking soldiers in such a situation is morally preferable, since they at least have the means to defend themselves. But is it right? In all probability we will end up maintaining that in an unjust war, the belligerent privileges of the aggressor side are based solely on an excuse, which undermines the presumption here of moral equality among soldiers.

It thus seems that in principle, a person can defend himself or his fellow citizens and country in a just war without putting his life at actual potential risk, and in an unjust war, the fact that the soldier puts his life at risk doesn't even grant him the right to attack enemy soldiers. For other good reasons, we might deny disguised combatants the right to participate in a war against unjust aggressors in order to protect other civilians. We might also excuse soldiers in an unjust war and grant them belligerent privileges. But if a disguised combatant is excluded from fighting even an unjust aggressor, they will not be connected to a lack of potential self-sacrifice, and if a soldier is included in the war zone of even an unjust war, they will not be linked to a willingness to risk and self-sacrifice. Self-sacrifice as such shouldn't play any moral role. The theorists who question both sides of the argument reveal in a moral way the problematic connection between sacrifice and violence. This link seems to me essential to the act of war. The willingness to sacrifice doesn't only enable empirically the act of war; it gives it both psychological and wrong moral justification.

In addition to the psychological and moral connection between self-sacrifice and violence in war, there is perhaps a deeper existential tie between the two. War is a perverse, though powerful, form of confronting birth and death.[22] By risking their lives, soldiers earn their right to live. They become, through this baptism of fire, owners of their own lives. What was given to them at birth arbitrarily and without choice belongs to them now. In risking their lives they mock death, and in killing they own death by taking life; it is as if they work out the drama of rebirth and death in that same action.

Ludwig Wittgenstein kept a diary while serving as a soldier in the Austrian army during the First World War, and one particular extract speaks to this point. Having specifically requested the most dangerous spot on the front, he wrote: "Only then will the war really begin for me. And—maybe—even life. Perhaps nearness of death will bring me the light of life."[23] Such a romantic conception of rebirth and consecration when gazing into death's eyes is distant from the actual realities of war. Those who survive the sight of death in war are usually not purified or redeemed; they end up traumatized and scarred for life. Such an existential quest tends to cover the gruesome reality of war.

In an ordinary moral conflict, the capacity for sacrifice sets a limit on aggression and violence. In war, these two urges do not stand in conflict with one another; they actually reinforce each other. War, which merges these impulses, creates an inseparable tie between violence and sacrifice. It is as hard to imagine undoing this knot as it is to imagine eradicating war.

Sacrifice and the Political Bond

Origin narratives of states and political or religious communities sometimes refer to heroic sacrifices performed by the founding generation. Future generations are assumed to be burdened with the onus of that early sacrifice, which demands loyalty, since betraying it means retroactively stripping the sacrifice of meaning. A past sacrifice therefore can become a binding political constraint on present-day politicians. "How can we withdraw now when so many soldiers gave their lives in this war?" How often have we heard such views expressed when a political community debates whether to remain engaged in a military venture? A great deal is known about the irrationality that can beset a prudent decision maker because of an incapacity to cut his losses. Yet with the burden of an earlier sacrifice, the issue is not about withdrawing from a losing situation and maximizing utility but instead a concern about retroactive desecration—a different sort of sensibility and expectation.

Calvin offered a formulation about the binding nature of past sacrifice: "When those things which the prophets and apostles and other martyrs endured to uphold God's truth are set before us, we are that much more strengthened to cling to faith that we hold, which they sealed with their blood."[24] Sacrifice and martyrology played similar roles during the formation of Christian denominations in the early modern period, when Catholics, Protestants, and Anabaptists subjected to torture and death at their rivals' hands used this same argument. The Catholic Reginald Pole, for example, appealed to his cousin Henry the VIII after Henry's execution of Thomas More and John Fisher: "Can I let the idea pass or say that those who sustained hardship for the sake of the Church, and without recompense suffered death for the sake of the Church, did so for nothing? . . . Can I now either think to myself or utter in speech the notion that those men, after putting up with so many hardships and tribulations, squandered their lives without purpose for nothing? I cannot, prince, I cannot. Let all such impiety be far from me."[25]

In this struggle of martyrological claims and counterclaims, it proved difficult to reach a compromise that might have loosened the rigid denominational boundaries and led to a truce in the religious wars. Any such compromise would have been interpreted as a retroactive annulment of the earlier sacrifices. One historian of early modern Christian martyrdom summed up this condition:

> By dying for doctrines about which Christians disagreed, martyrs infused religious dispute with human urgency. Any compromise could unfold only "over their dead bodies" and the memory of their refusal to submit. . . . It would have dishonored the martyrs' deaths with the implicit retrospective judgment that they too, instead of persevering, should have saved themselves by dissembling. Ultimately, it would have denied that the teachings for which they had died were worth dying for.[26]

This context sheds light on a deep, tragic aspect of human action. The past is never a closed event; its meaning continues to unfold and retroactively change in relation to new developments. This is as true of personal life as it is of historical events. What is the meaning of an event like Israel's Six-Day War? Did the war give Israel territories to exchange for a peace agreement? Did the event put Israel in an intolerable state of occupation and demographic disaster? Time will tell. This open-endedness of the past means, in effect, something much more radical than the common claim that we don't control the future of our efforts, given our finitude and limits. Rather, it is a more daring assertion: whatever we accomplish in the past is at the mercy of future action. Future events, in other words, will define retroactively the meaning of what it is that we have done. (The retroactive transformation of the past's meaning should not be confused with postmodern relativism about history and facts. Pointing to the fragility of the past and its open-endedness need not entail denying reality. Even when each of us has independent access to what has happened, the meaning and interpretation of the facts change in relation to future events. And these future events become themselves facts.)

The importance of the institution of the promise becomes clear when set against this condition of the fragility of the past. Think for a moment about a deathbed promise in which a dying author who has completed a magnum opus asks a friend to pledge that he will make an effort to publish it. The retroactive meaning of the author's past is effectively at stake. He is essentially entrusting his friend with the meaning of the years that are gone.

In contract law, this feature of the promise is expressed in rulings concerning reliance costs. If *A* invested money relying on a contractual promise made by *B*, and *B* breached the contract, B must compensate A for the loss he incurred by relying on the promise. But what about the costs incurred by A prior to the contract—costs that became retroactively ineffectual because of B's breach? Is B responsible for compensating him for this loss?

An English court dealt with such a case. A production company was making a film for television. In preparation for filming, a director, designer, and stage manager were hired. The production company also hired a well-known and talented actor for a central role, effectively counting on him to hold the film together. After signing the contract, the actor discovered that his agent had booked him for a play, so he breached the contract. The production company couldn't find a proper replacement and sued the actor. The actor readily agreed to compensate the company for some of its costs—for example, for expenses incurred in renting a film location as well as the transportation costs for the equipment and cast. But he refused to pay the costs of the investments made prior to his contractual obligation, such as the money spent on the director and designer. He argued that these costs, because they were incurred prior to his signing, did not hinge on his promise. The court disagreed, however, and ordered him to reimburse the production company for all its expenses, including those incurred prior to his contract. The court ruled that when the actor entered into the contract, he had been entrusted with the responsibility for these prior costs. Through its ruling, the court endorsed the principle that promising is not only about securing the future but also about consolidating the past.

This feature of human life destabilizes what seems to be a closed, complete achievement; it casts the shadow of fragility backward from the future onto the past. Such an undoing of the past might be a source of hope as well. Constructing a teleological process backward is a way of transforming a failure into a constructive moment in someone's life. It is one of the subtlest features of Saint Augustine's *Confessions*. In Augustine's understanding, the practice of confession is not reduced to someone admitting a failure and agreeing to change his behavior in the future; it is rather a way of viewing one's past sins and failures as a road that leads to a deeper understanding and revelation. For Agustine, confession is a form of praise, and as a retrospective redescription, it clears the way for understanding the nature of repentance as an attempt at undoing the past. Such backward causality might be at the source of sin's undoing in Jewish conceptions of repentance, in which repentance is not only a way of achieving forgiveness but also of transforming the meaning of the past.[27]

Some human activity is marked by the fact that it is less vulnerable to such dependency on future actions. I am referring to occurrences of sheer pleasure that are, in essence, nonteleological. For the same reason that they are independent of future events, they leave no trace in the memory except for the desire to repeat them. They don't amount to anything, since they are completely closed and momentary, and yet they are immensely attractive because they are self-contained. The acquisition of a skill, for example, is cumulative. The skill is "there"; it can be activated, improved, and used. This is not the case with pleasure which is consumed. A skill, as an effective tool, can be lost as well. With a slight change in technology, with a transformation of public taste, a skill earned over years of labor might become completely redundant and unnecessary. The years devoted to acquiring the skill might become retroactively empty. Because it is inscribed and reactivated, a skill's effectiveness can be taken away, which is not the case with pleasurable events. Such events are not "there" anymore; they cannot therefore be taken or redirected. The Epicureans saw the greatest of all consolations in this feature of pleasure, and the memory of moments that cannot be taken is itself reassuring. But its weakness rests in its fleetingness, and since it is not inscribed, it cannot be revived but only repeated. The memory of pleasure is not akin to the pleasure itself; the memory of a good dinner, say, might be quite painful when you are hungry.

Yet even pleasure is vulnerable to retroactive emptying. Imagine enjoying a good meal and realizing afterward that it was intended for a hungry, poor orphan or contained human flesh. Even so, in comparison with other human endeavors, the fact that pleasure is consumed does give it an advantage and stability in confronting the future. It might be said that if a pleasure becomes inscribed in the way a skill does, it cannot be repeated. Its inscription creates a threshold, which then has to be surpassed. The stakes will need to be raised in order to feel the sensation again. It is at this point that pleasure becomes dependent for its own fulfillment on a cycle of deprivation. This happens with drugs; doses must be continually increased in order to feel the impact. It could also happen with sex. A pleasure that has a memory numbs our capacity to repeat it. In such a case, breaking the pattern of self-containment might lead someone down the road of self-destruction. It is as if we must make an impossible choice between the self-contained, which is rather shallow, and the teleological, which is potentially futile.[28]

Cultures and civilizations often respond to the past's fragility by erecting monuments, enacting practices, and canonizing texts that ensure the enduring temporality of their producers. These memorials are meant as time capsules for future generations—to announce that this particular group of people pursued goals beyond the maintenance of life itself, and that their lives were dedicated to a realm above what Hannah Arendt called "labor." Some warrior societies have attempted to make their mark on the past as well as the future and present by destroying such symbols of endurance. They seize control of a community's past by annihilating it, thus retroactively sabotaging efforts at attaining an enduring legacy. "*Even the dead* will not be saved from the enemy if he wins," Walter Benjamin wrote in his sixth thesis on the philosophy of history.[29] The colonial habit of moving the past treasures of colonized communities to the great urban museums of the empires constituted a subtler, but in a way no less barbaric practice. The empire conquered its colony's past by preserving it, but in a space that the empire also chose, as a form of entertainment for museum-goers and other admirers of the exotic in the metropole.

Economic investments, like pleasure, share that feature of closure when their only goal is profit maximization. Economists apply the "sunk-cost fallacy" toward that activity. If someone has bought a prepaid ticket to a movie that he then learns is boring, it would be irrational on his part to spend his time going to the film. He would be wasting his time as well as the money he had already spent. People's tendency to pursue a failed investment in order to save face manifests an irrational limit to their recognition that these investments are things of the past. Such investors ought to be only future-oriented. Closure makes sense only when we deal with investments that concern us solely for the profit they will yield down the road. In such a case, any investment is interchangeable with another, since in this sphere of activity the wish for coherence and continuity is totally ignored.

In the realm of activities and efforts that are teleological in nature, where their meaning is cumulative, there is an important reason to save the past by future actions. The maintenance and building of political realities is such a human project; it depends on a shared generational effort to sustain it. It is a worthwhile endeavor to struggle over the onus of past sacrifice. To dismiss such human attempts at continuity merely on the basis of a sunk-cost fallacy is to conflate the logic of economic activities driven by the rational profit-maximization calculation with other spheres of life. We are thus faced with a genuine problem: How do we assess the claims that past sacrifices make on us, in light of our power to retroactively annul them?

There are some good, complex reasons to free oneself from such a burden, and it is helpful to explore these justifications in order to assess the claim. One of the main markers of something endowed with intrinsic value is its worthiness of genuine sacrifice. Yet in its binding and destructive power, a past sacrifice might work in the opposite direction. In such a reversal, it is not the case that something of value deserves sacrifice; rather, it is the sacrifice that constitutes its intrinsic value and sacredness, by endowing it with that sort of ultimate meaning. This reversal, discussed above, has a destructive role in the life of a group or individual, creating misguided self-transcendence. While pressing the obligation of past sacrifice on the present generation, such false self-transcendence replicates itself across time. The sacrifice's binding power in the political realm is a particular instance of a general connection between giving and binding. The debt felt to parents' sacrifices might be the most powerful vehicle for cross-generational continuity, especially when the sacrifice is committed for the children's sake. How many sons and daughters are held captive to their future to a family business developed through sweat and sometimes blood? Or take the case of immigrants who uprooted themselves and transformed their lives so that their children could have a better future, and their children then seem to waste the opportunity. The pure gift becomes an impossible act, since it is the giving that binds.

Relying on the burden of a past sacrifice that might be devoid of meaning is the last resort of a tradition that has lost its inherent claim and weight. This tradition has to revert, in the end, to a seemingly manipulative yet effective claim, as if clinging—since the project as such has lost its raison d'être—to that form of burdening support. The past sacrifice is like the last yet most powerful card in the continuity of historical effort. Its power might be immediate, but it will not be able to carry the weight for long. If the person entrusted with the onus of a past, misguided sacrifice is alienated from its purpose and sense, he will have to enslave his life to redeem its meaning. He will feel only resentment and malice; he will be unable to live a serious and genuine life. The psychological and social force of such a claim is clear, but what about its normative power? We can determine the meaning of past efforts, but to what degree does this fact serve as a legitimate claim altogether?

A binary argument can presumably be made: If the cause itself is just and worthy, there is no need for the burden of a past sacrifice to serve as a normative claim; the cause carries its own weight. If it is an unjust cause, the fact of a past sacrifice does not rightly serve as a reason to continue the practice or effort. Sacrifice ought not to have any sanctifying function as such. If the cause is unworthy, it should be admitted honestly that the past sacrifice was deeply misguided, rather than maintained that there is any obligation to preserve its continuity. Therefore, there is no room between these two options— just and unjust causes—for a normative burden.

These options, however, don't exhaust the possible space for such an obligation. The claim can be directed at a sphere of life dedicated to upholding particular political and cultural forms of life that are neither just nor unjust. Such forms include political institutions, religious practices, and linguistic and artistic traditions—all of which provide the fabric for a rich, specific life. Members of such structures can conceivably be obligated to the past in a manner that is not overriding but still powerful. One central way in which membership in a particular tradition is expressed is through people assuming responsibility for the sacrifices of previous generations. In a society with no strong sense of tradition, though, people might not feel this burden applies to them. This highlights an important feature of the plausible obligation to a past sacrifice: *it is not impersonal*. It is predicated on a previous sense of belonging, such as among friends, as in the earlier example of the obligation to publish a manuscript written by a dying author. It is not an obligation to humans qua humans; it is a manifestation of a more complex relationship.

Abraham Lincoln's *Gettysburg Address* was a monumental expression of the onus of past sacrifice. At the end of the speech, Lincoln asserted, "It is rather for us to be here dedicated to the great task remaining before us—that from these honored dead we take increased devotion to that cause for which they gave the last full measure of devotion—that we here highly resolved that these dead shall not have died in vain—that this nation, under God, shall have a new birth of freedom—and that government of the people, by the people, for the people, shall not perish from the earth." Lincoln, who witnessed the enormous casualties caused by the American Civil War, which far exceeded anything he had expected, transformed and reinterpreted the meaning of sacrifice. In confronting the direct horrors of the war, he realized that such a sacrifice couldn't only be for the sake of the Union's preservation. For the sacrifice to make sense and be justified, Lincoln believed, the moral stakes had to be higher. The soldiers had sacrificed their lives for the sake of freedom, for the very possibility of the endurance of the political ideals of equality and democracy.

The first obligation to this sacrifice, therefore, was to bestow a greater meaning on it, to channel that ultimate act of devotion into a worthy cause. Given Lincoln's great influence over the course of the struggle, he held the retroactive capacity to redirect the sacrifice. He refused to sanctify the Union cause through the sacrifice; instead, Lincoln transformed the meaning of the battle, supplying a goal that seemed to him worthy of such sacrifice. In establishing that case, he paid tribute to the sacrifice, but moved a step further, toward a second obligation: the onus of the past sacrifice. The recognition of the sacrifice obligated his audience to continue the struggle so that "these dead shall not have died in vain."

The political attempt at raising the moral stakes of a previous sacrifice in order to pursue it further is quite common. President George W. Bush, following the debacle in Iraq and the loss of more then three thousand US lives, made both steps. When weapons of mass destruction were not found in Iraq, he upped the ante, claiming that the war aimed to bring democracy and freedom to that country. He then declared the burden of sacrifice the reason to pursue the mission. Referring to the fallen soldiers in Iraq, Bush said, "We owe them something. . . . We will finish the task that they gave their lives for."

Lincoln's reinterpretation seems plausible. The ambiguities in the goals of the American Civil War were there to begin with, and indeed it was in Lincoln's power to clarify and redirect the nature of past events. In Bush's case, the redefinition of the war's aim appears artificial and unachievable. Even more so, given the cost and the future price, the constituency that Bush was addressing, unlike Lincoln's, seemed not to identify with that cause as their cause. Lincoln's war was, after all, about the identity and future of the United States; his audience understood that goal as their goal. It was natural for them to locate themselves as members of that same tradition and thus assume the burden as theirs. A past sacrifice can be a genuine motivating force for a political purpose; it can serve manipulative and dangerous functions as well. The source of its danger lies in the sacrifice sanctifying something that is unworthy and then holding future generations captive to its lingering onus. A primordial sacrifice—not original consent—might become the strongest glue adhering individuals to a political project.

The State and the Sacrificial Stage

What is the relationship between self-sacrifice and the political order? What sort of self-sacrifice, if any, is rightly demanded of a citizen in order to establish and maintain the political order? Hobbes and Locke both described the proper political order as a considered assemblage of individuals who for rational reasons prefer the conditions of cooperation to the supposedly natural state of competition. Individuals give up something when they step into the political order: their natural right to judge and punish their fellow humans. Yet no sacrifice is involved in establishing the political order. Citizens grant the sovereign a monopoly over the legitimate use of violence to defend themselves from violent attack. Their entry into the political realm is more like a form of postponed gratification than a genuine sacrifice; it is driven by pure self-interest.

From this social contract view of the political order, the phenomenon of war between antagonistic states calls into question the rationality of establishing the political realm in the first place. Once war has been declared, the sovereign, whose purpose is supposedly to protect individual lives and rights, has instead created a more perilous condition for the citizenry. Interstate warfare consumes the very individuals whose welfare the states were constituted to protect, and the level of peril may supersede the danger experienced by prepolitical individuals in the state of nature. It is no wonder that both Hobbes and Locke had difficulty justifying the state's right to enforce military conscription.[30] As Hegel articulated the problem in his remarks on the social contract, if the business of the state is to protect and secure human life, it cannot demand the sacrifice of life: "An entirely distorted account of the demand for this sacrifice results from regarding the state as a mere civil society and from regarding its final end as only the security of individual life and property. This security cannot possibly be obtained by the sacrifice of what is to be secured—on the contrary."[31]

Whether the move from the natural state to the political one was in fact rational is difficult to say, given the bloody history of modern states. Humans never created a greater altar to Molech than the centralized state. The modern state's hunger for human sacrifice is insatiable. Yet to even question this shift presupposes a dubious assumption about the nature of the political bond. Hobbesian rational choice psychology is limited since it assumes that self-preservation and self-interest are the foundational political motivations. Although Hobbes understood that there would be a condition similar to the state of nature between competing sovereign states, he didn't realize that this would change the relationship of citizens to their own state. Each sovereign state would establish a sacrificial bond rather than one rooted in self-interest, since it would need to recruit its citizens to face the new and more lethal state of nature in the arena of interstate military competition.[32]

Hobbes's moral psychology of human motivation was more sophisticated than many commentators have realized. Hobbes recognized that humans are not motivated solely by self-interest, acknowledged the force of sacrifice for the sake of moral ideals or religious beliefs, and gave a full account of the power of humiliation and honor to distort pure self-interest. His intention was to base the political bond on self-interest, claiming that other motivations such as empathy are not solid or reliable enough to ensure the preservation of the mutual covenant. Moreover, he was deeply suspicious of the desire to transcend self-interest, considering such inclinations to be sources of strife and destructive of political life. Hobbes relied on what he took to be the more psychologically dependable and predictable (and politically manageable) force of self-interest. In this respect, Hobbes's intention was to repress and marginalize other human tendencies—at least as far as politics was concerned. The history of the modern state is in some ways a return of the repressed. In its demand for self-sacrifice, the centralized state manifests the vengeful eruption of the sacrificial desire that Hobbes everywhere attempted to marginalize.[33]

The social contract tradition is of course bigger than Hobbes, and also produced a quite different view according to which the political order is a stage on which the individual could transcend the realm of self-interest. Rousseau, who considered the entry into the political as a shift from an individual to a general will, offered the best articulation of this approach. The move into the political realm, for Rousseau, involves transforming human motivation from a self-centered craving to a concern with the commonwealth's good: "The passing from the state of nature to the civil society produces a remarkable change in man; it puts justice as a rule of conduct in the place of instinct, and gives his actions the moral quality they previously lacked." According to Rousseau, the lawgiver of such a political order has the following task:

> Whoever ventures on the enterprise of setting up a people must be ready, shall we say, to change human nature, to transform each individual, who by himself is entirely complete and solitary, into a part of a much greater whole, from which that same individual will then receive, in a sense, his life and his being. The founder of nations must weaken the structure of man in order to fortify it, to replace the physical and independent existence we have all received from nature with a moral and communal existence.[34]

In line with his notion of citizenship, Rousseau wrote in favor of conscription and defended the view that the state could make a legitimate claim on an individual's life. The relationship between religion and the state is, for Rousseau, not only about jurisdiction and laws. Religion and the state are inherently in tension with each other, since the state trespasses into the religious domain by postulating itself as the vehicle for ultimate self-transcendence, thus performing a quasi-religious function.

These two distinct approaches also provide a different account of the way in which the political order relates to the problem of security and death. Hobbes assumed that the primary psychological motivation underlying the political is the attempt to avoid the ongoing possibility and fear of an early, violent death. Rousseau's contrary perspective is susceptible to another concern: overcoming death as opposed to avoiding it. The modern state, as a meaning endowing sacrificial community, allowed individuals to locate their life beyond the finite constraints of their own life span. If it is the case, as Rousseau argued, that in entering the political state the individual's identity is constituted by the "we" through internalizing the concern for other citizens as his concern, then individuals become part of an ongoing project, cutting across generations.[35] The urge to overcome death altogether, as a fundamental political concern, might be far greater than the urge to delay it. Or put in more general terms, rational choice theory's failure in relation to the political realm stems from its general blindness to the nature of human motivation. The quest to transcend self-interest might be equally strong in forming the political bond as the desire to preserve self-interest.

It is important to clarify this Rousseauian notion of self-transcendence. One can ground a concern for others' well-being in different ways. The first way is instrumental, when it is in the individual's self-interest to be concerned with the well-being of others, if such concern is reciprocated. No self-transcendence is involved in this motivational structure. Such instrumental contentions are scattered throughout Rousseau's writings in support of the restrictions imposed on the private will in taking responsibility for the general will. Yet Rousseau seemed to argue for the adoption of others' well-being for its own sake. Rousseau went even further, following a third path, when he claimed that after joining the political realm, the concern for the well-being of all citizens becomes constitutive of one's individual identity.[36] This third sense appears to recall the experience of parents whose sacrifices for their children are sometimes understood not as a sacrifice of self-interest for the other's sake but instead as constitutive of their identity as persons. In radical cases, this identity might exhaust their sense of being, and giving to their children consumes their identity. In adopting such a view, parents move from being people who make sacrifices to becoming sacrificing parents.

In positing a shift from instrumentally to noninstrumentally motivated concern for the other, to constitutive forms, Rousseau associated self-transcendence—the founding moment of the political order—with freedom. The individual regains his truer, deeper self by giving himself completely to the general will. Rousseau's description of the social contract is saturated with this kind of appeal: "Man acquires with civil society, moral freedom, which alone makes man the master of himself; for to be governed by appetite alone is slavery while obedience to a law one prescribes to oneself is mastery."[37] In their natural state, humans were driven by self-interest and raw empathy; their condition, though rudimentary, was morally tolerable. But in due course, when social reality was formed and humans didn't live the solitary life of the natural state, self-interest gained a destructive edge. As humans internalized a view of the other as the source of self-esteem, their self-interest became both comparative and competitive.

If humans had managed to stay in self-enclosed primary units such as the family, they might have avoided the horrible impact of society. Yet in their almost-irreversible movement away from the natural state, humans found themselves in an intolerable social and pre-citizenship stage. People worked their way out of this social malaise by entering into a full life of equal, free citizenship. They regained their freedom by adopting the common good as the prime motivator in citizens' lives.[38] The life of citizenship is thus the framework that allows for a radical shift in the nature of human motivation, from self-regarding to the adoption of the common good, and according to Rousseau, this in turn permits humans to gain what he called moral freedom.

The deep influence of this idea on Kant's moral philosophy is evident and known. Kant identified duty with freedom, since in acting from duty we move from the causal, natural realm of our conditional self-centered motivation to the realm of the autonomous free will. Rousseau perceived the social contract as a solution to the following concern: "To find a form of association . . . under which each individual, while uniting himself with the others, obeys no one but himself, and remains as free as before."[39] Building on Rousseau's statement, Kant modeled his conception of the kingdom of ends: "A rational being belongs as a member of the kingdom of ends when he gives universal laws in it but is also himself subject to these laws."[40] Yet the difference between Rousseau and Kant reveals the difficulties in viewing the political realm as the arena of self-transcendence. Rousseau's general will is understood to consist in the common good of the other citizens in the body politic.[41] It is neither synonymous with humanity as such, nor comparable to some imagined community of all rational creatures, as in Kant's moral theory. Kant saved the general will from this Rousseauian parochialism by shifting the locus of the sacrificial act from the general will of the political state to the categorical universal imperative, thereby preventing the notion from degenerating into a chauvinistic form of collective self-regard. Kant rescued this theme from its idolatrous implication.

While embracing the significance of self-transcendence to the moral life, I tried in this chapter to explore the inner tensions that arise in the movement of the self to self-transcendence. Shifting our perspective to this realm of problems exposes a different approach to moral conflict, in which misdirected self-transcendence is at least as problematic for the moral life as overindulgence is for self-interest. The nexus of self-sacrifice and violence, which reaches its peak in war, is the clearest manifestation of such a possible tension. In war, this stress is revealed not only as a psychological existential condition but also in how political theorists and lawyers constitute the morality of war.

This emergent tension in the realm of moral conflict becomes crucial to politics when it is acknowledged that in the creation of the political bond, the quest for self-transcendence plays at least as important a role as the urge for self-interest. The state provides a critical stage of self-transcendence, and as such political life might be prone to the sort of anxieties that arise in the moral drama in general. Citizens' commitment to sacrifice their interests for the sake of their fellow citizens is an admirable aspect of political association. It has to show itself not only in the joint effort of self-defense among citizens but also in a willingness to share the fruits of common labor between citizens, in the form of a greater egalitarian concern and solidarity with the plight of the weak and vulnerable. When the state becomes the sole locus of self-transcendence, however, it turns into a false idol.

There should be a realm beyond such a sacrificial stage that sets a higher, limiting standard for the political association. Different traditions will articulate that realm in different ways, from human rights that ought to limit state interests, to the image of God that all humans are supposed to share regardless of their associational affinities. A political body that lacks such a category directs the sacrificial urge to an unworthy cause. An absolute commitment to an unworthy cause is the modern form of the old problem of idolatry.

Conclusion

❧

Sacrifice is an essential phenomenon of religious, ethical, and political life. In its two senses, as "sacrificing to" and "sacrificing for," the linguistic use of the term covers immensely diverse experiences. It touches on ritual, atonement, substitution, self-transcendence, war, the responsibility to the past, and the state. Yet there is something at the core of this varied, rich phenomenon that justifies the use of the same word to express both meanings in so many languages. The term has to do with the identification of the sacrifice with the noninstrumental realm. In its mode as an offering, "sacrificing to" is an attempt to establish a bond of solidarity and love that transcends the logic of market exchange. The offering, as distinct from payment, is supposed to be part of the relationship, not the reason for it. Like all such attempts it is in constant danger of collapsing into a market exchange, especially when it is constituted, as an offering, as part of a hierarchical order of dependency. In its mode as "sacrificing for," the sacrifice *of* the self is an effort to act above and beyond self-interest, aiming at the realm of self-transcendence. It is for this reason that the human capacity to give up and sacrifice self-interest for the sake of another human or an ideal seems, to many people, a constitutive dimension of the moral life as such.

A common feature of this diverse phenomenon is violence. In "sacrificing to," three contexts of violence were identified: the violent response to rejection that stems from the inherent gap between giving and receiving in the act of the offering; the tormenting trial that emerges from the anxiety of instrumentality in the quest for love within the asymmetry of power; and most important, the violence that is directed toward the essentially innocent substitute at the basic structure of atonement. As I pointed out earlier, post-sacrificial religions are supposed to resolve atonement's cruel paradox by placing affliction at the center of atonement. When suffering atones, there is a deep shift in the direction of substitution. Another innocent subject no longer represents the sinner and accepts his punishment; rather, the locus of substitution is a symbolic punishment directed at the sinner himself.

This shift, which might have served a crucial role in extending the concept of "sacrificing to" to "sacrificing for," sets a whole new stage for the relationship between sacrifice and violence. Here too, within the realm of "sacrificing for," three contexts of violence emerged: with sacrifice, an unjust cause might be sanctified by a reversal in the causal order, from the justified claim that valuable things are worthy of sacrifice to the assertion that what was sacrificed for is itself of value; self-sacrifice also can serve as a lethal reversal of aggressor and victim, in which the aggressor perceives himself as the "true" victim of his own crime when his crime involves self-sacrifice; and mostly, when the quest for self-transcendence is recruited for an unworthy and misguided cause, it becomes an impetus for widespread destruction.

The modern history of the state as the locus of the sacrificial quest is testimony to this form of perversion. In positing itself as a sacrificial stage and the genuine realm of noninstrumental action, the state threatens to exhaust and monopolize the realm of the transcendent. It thus becomes a false god, providing the loyal citizen a misdirected sense of redemption from his selfish cage. Contemporary structures of violence combined with suicide perform two lethal reversals as well: the reversal from perpetrator to victim, and the reversal of the causal order between sacredness and devotion. The exploration of "sacrificing for" reveals that much of the moral and political drama is therefore set not in the clash between self-interest and self-transcendence but rather in the dark side of the noble quest for the realm of the noninstrumental and self-transcendent.

Notes

ᏮᎧ

PART I: SACRIFICING TO

1. See the formulation in Guy G. Stroumsa, *The End of Sacrifice: Religious Transformations in Late Antiquity* (Chicago: University of Chicago Press, 2009), 72–73.

2. For a critique of the uncovering of sacrifice's origin, see John Milbank, "Stories of Sacrifice: From Wellhausen to Girard," *Theory, Culture, and Society* 12, no. 4 (November 1995): 15–46. See also Burton Mack, introduction to *Violent Origins: Walter Burkert, René Girard, and Jonathan Z. Smith on Ritual Killing and Cultural Formation*, ed. Robert G. Hamerton-Kelly (Stanford, CA: Stanford University Press, 1987), 10–12.

3. Another term that designates sacrifice—though not in the sense of offering, such as *korban* or *minchah*—is *zevach*. *Korban* is used to denote an offering in general, not only an animal offering brought to God. For example, when the chieftains brought offerings for the dedication of the tabernacle, the term *korban* is used to describe gifts such as silver bowls and basins: "The one who presented his offering [*korbano*] on the first day was Nahshon son of Amminadab of the tribe of Judah. His offering [*korbano*]: one silver bowl weighing 130 shekels and one silver basin of 70 shekels" (Num. 7:12–13). The term *zevach*, on the other hand, is strictly reserved for occasions of ritual slaughtering such as ritual meals or animal offerings brought to the temple, usually shared by the one who brings the offering in opposition to the *olah*, which designates an offering totally consumed at the altar. It is important to emphasize that in contrast to the *zevach*, within the technical language of the priestly material the verb *le-hakrib* doesn't indicate the slaughtering of the animal but instead bringing it forward. (This is manifested, for example, in Lev. 1:3–5.) The *korban* therefore is not the object that was slaughtered but rather the object that was brought forward and offered. It is for

this reason that *korban* can refer to the offering of vessels to the temple. Being almost a technical term for a subset of sacrifices, the term *zevach* can't be used as a linguistic key to reveal the meaning of the phenomenon of sacrifice as a whole.

4. Marcel Mauss, *The Gift: The Form and Reason for Exchange in Archaic Societies* (London: Routledge Classics, 2002).

5. See Raymond Firth, "Offering and Sacrifice: Problems of Organization," *Journal of the Royal and Anthropological Institute of Great Britain and Ireland* 93, no. 1 (January–June 1963): 12–13.

6. A strong philological support for the centrality of the gift in sacrifice is revealed from the analysis of the term *ishe*, which is commonly used in describing the sacrifice. Jacob Milgrom, on the basis of the Akkadian meaning of the word, translates *ishe* as a gift. See Jacob Milgrom, *The Anchor Bible: Leviticus 1–16* (New York: Doubleday, 1991), 161–62.

7. An interesting similar reversal of the direction of the gift appears in Lev. 17:11. In this verse, the claim is made that humans are not the ones who give the blood of the sacrifice to God; God has given it on the altar for their sake. The blood of the sacrificed animal given by the offerer is actually God's gift to them. This point is made by Baruch J. Schwartz, "Prohibition concerning the 'Eating' of the Blood," in *Priesthood and the Cult in Ancient Israel*, ed. Gary A. Anderson and Saul M. Olyan (Sheffield, UK: Sheffield Academic Press, 1991), 50–51.

8. Chapter 17 in Leviticus postulates that meat originating from animals that can be sacrificed should be eaten only when those animals are brought as an offering to the altar. Unlike the gift cycle that operates in offering the first fruits, the gift cycle in the case of consuming meat is far stricter and less symbolic. The one who consumes meat can only do it after offering the animal to God, since the killing of such an animal is prohibited unless it was brought to God, who owns its life and returns portions of it to the one who wishes to eat meat.

9. See the Platonic dialogue *Euthyphro* and Socrates' criticism of the understanding of sacrifice as a form of material exchange. See also the defense of the sacrifice by the pagan Sallust in Arthur Darby Nock, *Sallustius: Concerning the Gods and the Universe* (Cambridge: Cambridge University Press, 1926), 139.

10. W. Robertson Smith, *Lectures on the Religion of the Semites: The Fundamental Institutions* (London: Adam and Charles Black, 1927).

11. Smith's chronology depends on the dating of the priestly source as later postexilic stratum of the text—an assumption that was challenged in Yehezkel Kaufmann, *History of the Israelite Religion* (Tel Aviv: Dvir, 1955), 2:532–88 (Hebrew); Israel Knohl, *The Sanctuary of Silence: The Priestly Torah and the Holiness School* (Minneapolis: Fortress Press, 1995), 41–45; Jacob Milgrom, "The Antiquity of the Priestly Source: A Replay to Joseph Blenkinsopp," *Zeitschrift für die Alttestamentliche Wissenschaft* 111, no. 1 (January 1999): 10–22. For an assessment of Smith's views and the anthropologically relevant material, see Robert Alun Jones, "Robertson Smith, Durkheim, and Sacrifice: An Historical Context for the 'Elementary Forms of Religious Life,'" *Journal of the History of the Behavioral Sciences* 17, no. 2 (April 1981): 184–205.

12. See George B. Gray, *Sacrifice in the Old Testament: Its Theory and Practice* (New York: Ktav, 1971). For a critique of Smith's marginalization of the gift in sacrifice and his misunderstanding of the gift's function, see John Milbank, "Stories of Sacrifice: From Wellhausen to Girard," *Theory, Culture, and Society* 12, no. 4 (November 1995): 22.

13. For a more nuanced symbolic understanding of reception that implies not literal feeding but rather consuming, see Jonathan Klawans, *Purity, Sacrifice, and the Temple: Symbolism and Suppression in the Study of Ancient Judaism* (Oxford: Oxford University Press, 2006), 44.

14. In response to Smith's explanation, which produces an unnecessarily strict division between the gift and communion, Émile Durkeim pointed out the connection between these two functions. See Émile Durkheim, *The Elementary Forms of the Religious Life: A Study in Religious Sociology*, trans. Joseph W. Swain (London: George Allen and Unwin, 1968), 341–43.

15. I find Mauss's work on the gift far more illuminating on the issue of sacrifice within the biblical tradition than his own account of sacrifice in Henri Hubert and Marcel Mauss, *Sacrifice: Its Nature and Function*, trans. W. D. Halls (Chicago: University of Chicago Press, 1964). Hubert and Mauss argue that sacrifice is a form of

communication between the profane and sacred worlds, in which the sacrifice modifies the status of the person who performs it. Such a person is transformed to the sacred realm through the intermediary of the sacrifice, which is a consecrated thing that is destroyed in the process. In my opinion, the biblical material doesn't attest to such a transformation of the offerer's condition, and this absence is affirmed by the lack of desacralization procedures in the biblical material—essential to the thesis introduced by Hubert and Mauss.

16. The second sacrifice recorded in the Bible after Cain's and Abel's reflects another attempt at securing a stable future independent of the ongoing, unexpected gift cycle. After Noah was saved from the flood, he made a sacrifice to God from the pure animals he had taken with him on the ark. It was an offering of gratitude in which the sacrificed animals stood for the lives that were saved and then returned symbolically to God. God, who was pleased with the sacrifice, made a covenant, vowing not to destroy the universe as he had tried to do in the flood:

> Then Noah built an altar to the Lord and, taking of every clean animal and of every clean bird, he offered a burnt offering on the altar. The Lord smelled the pleasing odor, and the Lord said to Himself: "Never again will I doom the earth because of man, since the devisings of man's mind are evil from his youth; nor will I ever again destroy every living being as I have done." . . . And God said to Noah and to his sons with him, "I now establish My covenant with you and your offspring to come, and with every living thing that is with you—birds, cattle, and every wild beast as well—all that have come out of the ark every living thing on earth. I will maintain My covenant with you: never again shall all flesh be cut off by the waters of a flood, and never again shall there be a flood to destroy the earth." God further said, "This is a sign that I set for the covenant between Me and you, and every living creature with you, for all ages to come. I have set My bow in the clouds and it shall serve as a sign of covenant between Me and the earth." (Gen. 8:20–21, 10:8–13)

The existence of the universe was secured forever due to one successful sacrificial act. The world's future was now independent from its ongoing maintenance by a ritual meant to maintain the gift cycle.

Its future was secured through the oath and covenant evoked by one sacrifice—Noah's sacrifice after the flood.

17. A similar approach is expressed in the Talmud warning against prolonging prayer, and the fact that such a practice might cause the petitioners' sins to be recorded. See Babylonian Talmud, Berakhot 55a.

18. The prophetic critique of sacrifice is not an opposition to ritual as such. Rather, it is a rejection of the presumption that it can be accepted independent of the moral and religious status of the one who brings the offering.

19. For his analysis of the role of sacrifice and its function as a scapegoat, see René Girard, *Violence and the Sacred*, trans. Patrick Gregory (Baltimore: Johns Hopkins University Press, 1977); René Girard, *Job: The Victim of His People*, trans. Yvonne Freccero (Stanford, CA: Stanford University Press, 1987); René Girard, *Things Hidden since the Foundation of the World*, trans. Stephen Bann and Michael Metter (Stanford, CA: Stanford University Press, 1987).

20. On the relationship between violence and humiliation, see James Gilligan, *Violence: Our Deadly Epidemic and Its Causes* (New York: Putnam, 1996).

21. For the meaning of accepting or giving willingly *le-ratzon* as wholehearted joyful acceptance, see Milgrom, *The Anchor Bible*, 150–51; Yochanan Muffs, *Love and Joy: Law, Language, and Religion in Ancient Israel* (New York: Jewish Theological Seminary of America, 1992), chapters 7–8. See also the analysis of this terminology in Gary A. Anderson, *Sin: A History* (New Haven, CT: Yale University Press, 2009), 51–54.

22. I am translating the term *min-haadamah* as "from the land," rather than as "more than the land," as in the Jewish Publication Society's translation. I am following Nahmanides in his commentary on Genesis 4:11.

23. On the centrality of the sacrifice as a stand-in for the sacrifice of the son, see Jon D. Levenson, *The Death and Resurrection of the Beloved Son: The Transformation of Child Sacrifice in Judaism and Christianity* (New Haven, CT: Yale University Press, 1993). Within the context of love, such substitution reveals a tension, as pointed out in Brian K. Smith and Wendy Doniger, "Sacrifice and Substitution: Ritual Mystification and Mythical Demystification," *Numen* 36, no. 2 (December 1989): 189–224. Sacrifice can be performed

only as a substitute; if unmediated by the substitute, sacrifice entails murder and the destruction of love. How could Abraham continue to love God if he would have sacrificed Isaac, knowing that the demand was motivated by God's self-doubt? On the other hand, sacrifice as a substitute ends up being negated in the attempt to establish it as principle, since it is, after all, only a substitute.

24. Pierre Bourdieu, *Algeira 1960* (Cambridge: Cambridge University Press, 1979), 22.

25. See David Cheal, *The Gift Economy* (London: Routledge, 1988).

26. I am indebted to the anonymous reader of the manuscript for this insight concerning the diversity of divine images that emerges in these stories.

27. Milgrom developed this conception of atonement in a variety of places. See Jacob Milgrom, *Studies in Levitical Terminology* (Berkeley: University of California Press, 1970); Jacob Milgrom, *Studies in Cultic Theology and Terminology* (Leiden: Brill, 1983), 96–103. For an extensive bibliography on the analysis of the term, see Baruch J. Schwartz, "Prohibition concerning the 'Eating' of the Blood," in *Priesthood and the Cult in Ancient Israel*, ed. Gary A. Anderson and Saul M. Olyan (Sheffield, UK: Sheffield Academic Press, 1991), 51n3.

28. According to Levine, the very approach before God requires atonement. Therefore, in every sacrifice, even when not aimed at atonement, the blood will serve as a protective substitute. See the Jewish Publication Society's translation of Leviticus (Philadelphia, 1989, 115): "The sacrifice substituted for an individual human life or for the lives of the member of the community in situations where God could have exacted the life of the offender, or of anyone else, for that matter. Indeed, all who stood in God's immediate presence risked becoming the object of divine wrath. But the substitution could avert the danger, with sacrificial blood being especially instrumental because it was the symbol of life."

29. For a discussion of this phenomenon, see George Fletcher, *The Grammar of Criminal Law* (Oxford: Oxford University Press, 2007), 119–31.

30. This leads to a possible speculation. In Hebrew, the merging of the sacrifice and victim happened quite late, in the second half of the twentieth century. It took place much earlier in languages that de-

veloped within the Christian tradition, because of the way in which
an offering and victimhood were combined at the crucifixion.

31. For this reason, there is an attempt in the scapegoat tradition
to ascribe voluntariness to the victim. See the Greek texts mentioned
in Walter Burket, *Homo Necans: The Anthropology of Ancient Greek
Sacrificial Ritual and Myth*, trans. Peter Bing (Berkeley: University
of California Press, 1983), 10n4. These sources attest to animals
that voluntarily offer themselves up as sacrifices. See Jan N. Brem-
mer, "Scapegoat Rituals in Ancient Greece," in *Oxford Readings
in Greek Religion*, ed. Richard Buxton (Oxford: Oxford University Press, 2000), 279–80. See also Origen, *Contra Celsum* 1:31:
"They [the apostles] not only dared to show to the Jews from
the words of the prophets that he was [the] prophesied one, but
also to the other peoples that he, who had been recently crucified voluntarily died for mankind, like those who died for their fatherland,
to avert plague epidemics, famines and shipwreck." The Midrash,
in its attempt to explain why only domestic animals rather than
wild ones offer themselves as sacrifices, quotes the verse stating that
God seeks the persecuted. Sacrifice is described in this text not as
violence enacted on the innocent animal but instead as bringing
the animal closer to God by virtue of its innocence. See Leviticus
Rabba 27:5.

32. "In her Magisterial teaching of the faith and in the witness of
her saints, the Church has never forgotten that sinners were the au-
thors and the ministers of all the sufferings that the divine Redeemer
endured. Taking into account the fact that our sins affect Christ himself, the Church does not hesitate to impute to Christians the gravest
responsibility for the torments inflicted upon Jesus, a responsibility
with which they have all too often burdened the Jews alone: We must
regard as guilty all those who continue to relapse into their sins.
Since our sins made the Lord Christ suffer the torment of the cross,
those who plunge themselves into disorders and crimes crucify the
Son of God anew in their hearts (for he is in them) and hold him up
to contempt. And it can be seen that our crime in this case is greater
in us than in the Jews. As for them, according to the witness of the
Apostle, 'None of the rulers of this age understood this; for if they
had, they would not have crucified the Lord of glory.' We, however,
profess to know him. And when we deny him by our deeds, we in
some way seem to lay violent hands on him. Nor did demons crucify

him; it is you who have crucified him and crucify him still, when you delight in your vices and sins" (catechism of the Catholic Church, section 598).

33. On the theme of God's own sacrifice, see Kimberley C. Patton, *Religion of the Gods: Ritual, Paradox, and Reflexivity* (Oxford: Oxford University Press, 2009). For an illuminating discussion of a divine being offering to himself in the Christian tradition, see 240–47.

34. On the relationship between charity and sacrifice as it was located within the metaphor of sin as a debt, see the insightful discussion in Gary A. Anderson, *Sin: A History* (New Haven, CT: Yale University Press, 2009), chapters 9, 11. On the particular reading of the verse in Proverbs, see 165–67, 221n18.

35. Jacob Z. Lauterbach, ed., *Mechilta tractate Bahodesh*, 280.

36. See Pesikta de-Rav Kahanah, Shuva 5; Babylonian Talmud, Sanhedrin 43b.

37. On the death penalty as an atoning process, see Mishnah Sanhedrin 6:2. On lashes, see Makot 3:17.

38. For the purpose of atonement, a far greater role for self-imposed suffering was offered in the literature of medieval Ashkenazic piety and its followers. See Ivan G. Marcus, *Piety and Society: The Jewish Pietists of Medieval Germany* (Leiden: Brill, 1981). On the subsequent influence of pietists in Ashkenaz, see Jacob Elbaum, *Repentance and Self-Flagellation in the Writings of the Sages of Germany and Poland, 1348–1648* (Jerusalem: Magnes Press, 1992) (Hebrew).

39. See Saul Lieberman in his edition of the Tosefta. He explains that in this text, Yom Kippur refers to fasting, since when describing suffering in the third category it mentions suffering the rest of the year—meaning that pain is added to the suffering that happens on Yom Kippur.

40. When substitution becomes an option, then the following process might be operative: substitutes are created for what was before a substitute. The rabbinic material views the death penalty as a substitute for a harsher penalty: loss of life after death altogether. Rabbi Ishmael devised the next stage of substitution: when suffering substituted for the penalty of execution, which was already considered a substitute. The court, by making use of the death penalty,

symbolically preempts a harsher punishment that might be given by God, and in turn, God symbolically preempts a hasher punishment that might be given by the court.

41. See Babylonian Talmud, Berakhot 26b. For the emergence of prayer as a structured daily obligation after the destruction of the temple, see Ezra Fleischer, "On the Beginnings of Obligatory Hebrew Prayer," *Tarbiz* 59 (1990): 397–441 (Hebrew).

42. The idea of prayer as an actual offering is present in the Dead Sea Scrolls prior to its emergence in the rabbinic material. In the second and first centuries BC, members of the Judean Desert Sects established an alternative to temple worship while the temple was still intact, since they regarded worship at the temple as defiled, and based on the wrong calendar and practices. The main mode of substitution for the temple was prayer, which according to the writings of the Dead Sea Sects, emulates the worship of the angels in the heavenly temple—worship consisting of hymns of praise given to God as verbal offerings. On that theme, see Bilha Nitzan, *Qumran Prayer and Poetry* (Jerusalem: Bialik Institute, 1996), 212–20 (Hebrew). On the general theme of the heavenly temple and its emulation in the life sect, see Rachel Elior, *Temple and Chariot, Priests and Angels, Sanctuary and Heavenly Sanctuaries in Early Jewish Mysticism* (Jerusalem: Magnes Press, 2007) (Hebrew).

43. See Letter to the Hebrews 13:15. See Robert J. Daly, *Christian Sacrifice: The Judaeo-Christian Background before Origen* (Washington, DC: Catholic University of America Press, 1978), 261–81.

44. This process was analyzed in Shlomo Naeh, "'Creates the Fruit of Lips': A Phenomenological Study of Prayer according to Mishnah Berakhot 4:3, 5:5," *Tarbiz* 63 (1994): 185–218 (Hebrew). On the image of prayer as offered fruits (*terumat sfataim*) in the Dead Sea Scrolls, see Bilha Nitzan, *Qumran Prayer and Poetry* (Jerusalem: Bialik Institute, 1996), 35–36 (Hebrew). In later reflections on prayer, the sense of offering in the act of prayer is sharpened as well as deepened by the claim that the posture implied by prayer itself is a form of offering. The petitioner surrenders his fate into God's hands, thereby renouncing his own autonomy and expressing his dependency; he offers his self in order to regain it.

45. For parallels, see Leviticus Rabba 9:1; Theodor/Albeck, ed., Genesis Rabba, section 97.

46. The medieval halakhists debated whether a person, in relation to all other obligations, is merely permitted not to give up his life or is prohibited from doing so. Maimonides ruled that a person who gave up his life when he was not obligated to do so is liable for prohibited suicide, while other medieval halakhists thought that such a person is allowed to give up his life or even praised when he gives up his life without any obligation to do so. On this debate along with its larger cultural and religious context, see Haym Soloveitchik, "Halakhah, Hermeneutics, and Martyrdom in Medieval Ashkenaz," *Jewish Quarterly Review* 94, no. 1 (Winter 2004): 77–108; no. 2 (Spring 2004): 278–99.

47. There is the genuine possibility here of a further, more principled claim that unlike murder and incest, when idolatry is performed under coercion, it is a null and void action; it doesn't constitute worship of another god, since such worship must be intentional. See, for example, Nahmanides' position in Hidushei ha-Ramban, Shabbat 72b, "*Ela mehaavah u-meirah.*"

48. The conceptual distinction between the source of obligation to give up life in the case of three grave transgressions and the obligation to sanctify God's name in public was suggested by Nahmanides in Milhamot Hashem "*ve-od,*" Sanhedrin 17b. Maimonides, on the other hand, seems to have collapsed the different categories, and considered the obligation to give up life and not to murder or commit incest as related to the obligation to sanctify God's name (Mishneh Torah, Hilkhot Yesodei ha-Torah 5:1–2).

49. On these conceptions of martyrdom in the rabbinic tradition and their possible emergence within the Christian and Jewish discourse of martyrdom, see Daniel Boyarin, *Dying for God: Martyrdom and the Making of Christianity and Judaism* (Stanford, CA: Stanford University Press, 1999), 91–130. For an attempt to locate Christian martyrdom within the Roman context, see G. W. Bowersock, *Martyrdom and Rome* (Cambridge: Cambridge University Press, 1995).

50. For such rare mentions of an offering in relation to martyrdom, see Genesis Rabba, 34:21; Babylonian Talmud, Sanhedrin 110b.

51. Epistle to the Romans, chapter 4.

52. For this new dimension of martyrdom in the Christian tradition, see Guy G. Stroumsa, *The End of Sacrifice: Religious Transformations in Late Antiquity* (Chicago: University of Chicago Press,

2009), 75–77. See also J. Petruccione, "The Martyr Death as Sacrifice: Prudentius, Peristephanon 4. 9–72," *Vigiliae Christianae* 49, no. 3 (August 1995): 245–57.

53. This process is analyzed in clarity and detail in Ra'anan Boustan, *Martyr to Mystic: Rabbinic Martyrology and the Making of Merkavah Mysticism* (Tübingen: Mohr Siebeck, 2005), chapter 4.

54. Aharon Jellinek, ed., *Bet ha-Midrash*, book 2, 66; book 6, 22 (Jerusalem, 1967).

55. See, for example, Abraham Meir Haberman, ed., *Gzerot Askenaz ve-Zarfat* (Jerusalem 1971), 31, 49.

56. See ibid., 123. In his attempt to cast the martyrs' death in sacrificial terms, Ephraim of Buna is careful to use the verb *hiza* (sprinkled) rather than *shafach* (spilled), since this verb is used solely within the sacrificial rite of sprinkling the blood of the sacrificed animal on the altar. For the sacrificial theme in Ashkenazic martyrdom and its relationship to earlier traditions of the binding of Isaac, see Shalom Spiegel, *The Last Trial: On the Legends and Lore of the Command to Abraham to Offer Isaac as a Sacrifice—The Akedah*, trans. Judah Goldin (New York: Pantheon Books, 1967); Shalom Spiegel, "Me-Aggadot ha-Akedah—From the Legends of the Aggadah: A Piyyut on the Slaughter of Isaac and His Resurrection by Rabbi Ephraim of Bonn," in *Alexander Marx, Jubilee Volume*, ed. Saul Lieberman (New York: Jewish Theological Seminary of America, 1950), 471–547 (Hebrew); Shalom Spiegel, "In Monte Dominus Videbitur: The Martyrs of Blois and the Early Accusations of Ritual Murder," in *Mordecai M. Kaplan, Jubilee Volume*, ed. Moshe Davis (New York: Jewish Theological Seminary of America, 1953), 267–87 (Hebrew); Shalom Spiegel, "A Fragment from the Legends of the Akedah," in *Abraham Weiss, Jubilee Volume*, ed. Samuel Belkin (New York, 1964), 553–66 (Hebrew).

Part II: Sacrificing for

1. See, for example, Kant's formulation in Immanuel Kant, *Critique of Practical Reason* (1788; repr., Cambridge: Cambridge University Press, 1997), 5:83–84. For the place of sacrifice in moral life, see Joseph Raz, "The Central Conflict: Morality and Self-Interest," in *Engaging Reason: On the Theory of Value and Action* (Oxford: Oxford University Press, 1999), 303–32.

2. See Bernard Williams, "A Critique of Utilitarianism," in *Utilitarianism: For and Against*, ed. J. J. C. Smart and Bernard Williams (Cambridge: Cambridge University Press, 1982), 77–150.

3. See Sam Scheffler, *Human Morality* (Oxford: Oxford University Press, 1992).

4. See Liam Murphey, *Moral Demands in Nonideal Theory* (Oxford: Oxford University Press, 2000).

5. Himmler's speeches are quoted in Hannah Arendt, *Eichmann in Jerusalem: A Report on the Banality of Evil* (New York: Penguin Books, 1994), 105.

6. Ibid.

7. Søren Kierkegaard, *Fear and Trembling* (London: Penguin Classics, 1986).

8. Both secular nationalists and religiously motivated people have adopted the strategy of suicide bombing. For an extensive analysis of this phenomenon, see Robert Pape, *Dying to Win: The Strategic Logic of Suicide Terrorism* (New York: Random House, 2005).

9. For one such common formulation, see Kant, *Critique of Practical Reason*, 5:34–36.

10. See Kant's formulations in Immanuel Kant, *Religion within the Limits of Reason Alone*, trans. Theodore M. Green and Hoyt H. Hudson (1793; repr., New York: Harper and Row, 1960), 32–33, 41–43.

11. See ibid., 23–24.

12. See Kant, *Critique of Practical Reason*, 5:23; Christine M. Krosgaard, *Creating the Kingdom of Ends* (Cambridge: Cambridge University Press, 1996), 58–59, 58–59, 74n52.

13. Paul Kahn, *Sacred Violence: Torture, Terror, and Sovereignty* (Ann Arbor: University of Michigan Press, 2008), 97.

14. See, for example, the formulation in Robert Fullinwider, "War and Innocence," *Philosophy and Public Affairs* 5, no. 1 (Fall 1975): 90–97.

15. Michael Walzer, *Just and Unjust Wars* (New York: Basic Books, 1997), 182. See also the discussion in Mark Ossil, *The End of Reciprocity* (Cambridge: Cambridge University Press, 2009), 21–23.

16. See Paul Kahn, "The Paradox of Riskless Warfare," *Philosophy and Public Policy Quarterly* 22, no. 3 (Summer 2002): 2–8.

17. Ibid., 127.

18. For an attempt to define the sense of duress that is experienced by soldiers in wars and the applicability of such an excuse, see Cheney Ryan, "Moral Equality, Victimhood, and the Sovereignty Symmetry Problem," in *Just and Unjust Warriors: The Moral and Legal Status of Soldiers*, ed. David Rodin and Henry Shue (Oxford: Oxford University Press, 2008), 131–52.

19. For the complexity of such excuses based on duress and ignorance, and the way in which it cannot be applied indiscriminately to a whole army, see Judith Lichtenberge, "How to Judge Soldiers Whose Cause Is Unjust," in *Just and Unjust Warriors: The Moral and Legal Status of Soldiers*, ed. David Rodin and Henry Shue (Oxford: Oxford University Press, 2008), 123–29.

20. David Rodin takes issue with self-defense analogies altogether. In his view, this reductive approach fails to explain legitimate war. Among other criticisms, his argument is based on the assumption that in war, there is symmetry between the soldiers, which is not the case with self-defense. See David Rodin, *War and Self-Defense* (New York: Oxford University Press, 2003), 178. See also Noam Zohar, "Collective War and Individualistic Ethics: Against the Conscription of 'Self-Defense,'" *Political Theory* 21, no. 4 (November 1993): 606–22. This perspective is aptly criticized in Jeff McMahan, "War as Self-Defense," *Ethics and International Affairs* 18, no. 1 (Winter 2004): 75–80.

21. Jeff McMahan has articulated the most sustained critique of the moral equivalence of soldiers on the battlefield. In his thorough argument, however, he doesn't consider what looks like a strong and serious defense of such a view: the associational commitment of soldiers to one another. See Jeff McMahan, *Killing in War* (Oxford: Oxford University Press, 2009).

22. See Paul Kahn, *Out of Eden: Adam and Eve and the Problem of Evil* (Princeton, NJ: Princeton University Press, 2007), chapter 5.

23. Quoted in Ray Monk, *Ludwig Wittgenstein: The Duty of Genius* (New York: Penguin Books, 1991), 138.

24. At the last section of John Calvin, *Brief Instruction against the Anabaptists*, ed. and trans. Benjamin Wirt Farley (Grand Rapids, MI: Baker Book House, 1982).

25. Reginald Pole, *De Unitate* (Rome: Anotnius Bladus, ca. 1538), fol. 1v.

26. Brad S. Gregory, *Salvation at Stake: Christian Martyrdom in Early Modern Europe* (Cambridge MA: Harvard University Press, 2000), 7.

27. See Babylonian Talmud, Yoma 86a.

28. Aristotle, in rejecting the Epicurean option, was aware of the fragility of the past, which he discussed in the tenth and eleventh chapters of *Nicomachean Ethics*, book 1.

29. Walter Benjamin, *Illuminations*, ed. Hannah Arendt, trans. Harry Zohn (New York: Schocken Press, 1969), 255.

30. See Thomas Hobbes, *Leviathan* (1651; repr., London: Penguin, 1968), chapter 14; John Locke, *Second Treatise of Civil Government* (1690; repr., Amherst, NY: Prometheus Books, 1986). On the liberal difficulty in justifying conscription, see George Kateb, *The Inner Ocean* (Ithaca, NY: Cornell University Press, 1992), chapter 7.

31. G. W. F. Hegel, *Hegel's Philosophy of Right*, trans. T. M. Knox (Oxford: Oxford University Press, 1967), 324.

32. For the depth of the sacrificial element in the making of the nation-state, see Paul Kahn, *Putting Liberalism in Its Place* (Princeton, NJ: Princeton University Press, 2005).

33. This phenomenon also impacts other emotions that the centralized state wishes to marginalize in its own realm, and yet it makes extensive use of that same repressed emotion in its relations with other states. The modern state is based on the repression of revenge honor and humiliation as driving forces in citizens' relations to one another. Honor cultures and revenge traditions will never allow the state to monopolize punishment and retribution. It is thoroughly humiliating and unmanly to complain to the police after one's daughter is raped. Men of honor take matters into their own hands. And yet, although some modern sociologists claim the shift away from honor cultures, honor and revenge are the markers of intrastate relationship. It is therefore more accurate to claim that individual or tribal honor gave way to the vicarious honor of the nation and state.

34. Jean-Jacques Rousseau, *The Social Contact*, trans. Maurice Cranston (London: Penguin, 1968), 64, 84–85.

35. Rousseau never mentioned the argument for the adoption of the constitutive identity of the "we" as a way of overcoming the finite, transient nature of the self. Hegel articulated this implication.

36. See Frederick Neuhouser, *Foundations of Hegel's Social Theory* (Cambridge, MA: Harvard University Press, 2000), 165–98.

37. Rousseau, *Social Contract*, 65.

38. See Judith N. Shklar, *Men and Citizens: A Study of Rousseau's Social Theory* (Cambridge, MA: Harvard University Press, 1985), 50.

39. Rousseau, *Social Contract*, 60.

40. Immanuel Kant, "Groundwork of the Metaphysics of Morals," in *Practical Philosophy*, ed. Mary J. Gregor (Cambridge: Cambridge University Press, 1996), 83.

41. See Jean-Jacques Rousseau, "The Discourse of Political Economy," in *The Social Contract and Discourses*, trans. G. D. H. Cole (London: Noah Publishing, 2003), 142–43.

Index

☙

Index